C000293000

IMAGES OF ENGLAND

STROUD STREETS
AND SHOPS

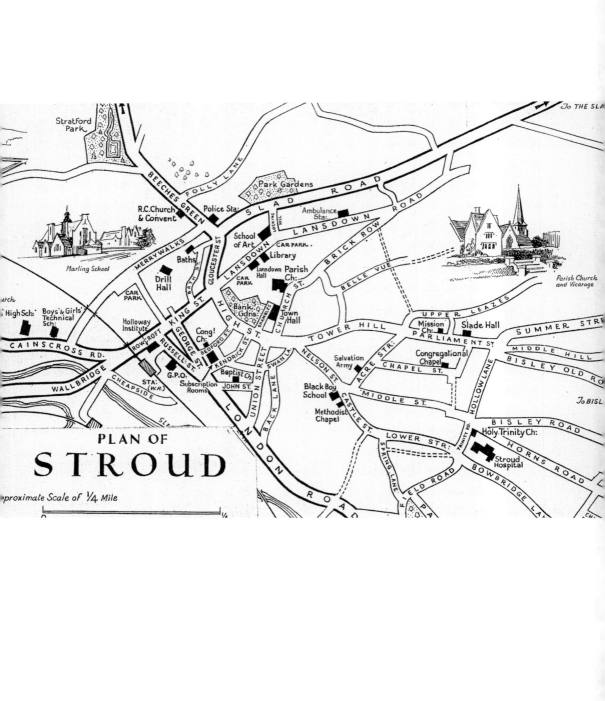

PLAN OF
STROUD

Approximate Scale of ¼ Mile

Stratford
Park

Folly Lane

Park Gardens

Beeches Green

R.C.Church
& Convent

Police Sta:

Slad Road

Locking Hill

Ambulance
Sta:

Lansdown Road

Brick Row

Marling School

Merry Walks

School
of Art

Library

Car Park

Parish Church
and Vicarage

Baths

Lansdown Road

Parish
Ch:

Belle Vue

Drill
Hall

Bath St.

Lansdown
Hall

Church St.

Upper Leazes

Car
Park

Gloucester St.

Summer Str

Car Park

High Sch:

Boys' & Girls'
Technical
Sch:

Holloway
Institute

King St.

High St.

Bank
Gdns.

Shambles

Town
Hall

Tower Hill

Mission
Ch:

Slade Hall

Middle Hill

Parliament St.

Bisley Old Ro

Cainscross Rd.

Rowcroft

Cong!
Ch:

George St.

Russell St.

Bedford St.

Kendrick St.

Union Street

Nelson St.

Salvation
Army

Congregational
Chapel

Acre Str.

Chapel St.

Bisley Road

To Bisl

Wallbridge

Cheapside

Sta.
(W.R.)

G.P.O.

Baptist Ch:

John St.

Swan La.

Back Lane

Subscription
Rooms

Black Boy
School

Middle St.

Hollow Lane

Methodist
Chapel

Castle St.

London Road

Lower Str.

Field Road

Spring Lane

Trinity Rd.

Holy Trinity Ch:

Bisley Road

Horns Road

Stroud
Hospital

Bowbridge La

To The Sla

IMAGES OF ENGLAND

STROUD STREETS AND SHOPS

WILF MERRETT

TEMPUS

Frontispiece: Map of Stroud, *c.* 1950.

First published 2004

Tempus Publishing Limited
The Mill, Brimscombe Port,
Stroud, Gloucestershire, GL5 2QG
www.tempus-publishing.com

© Wilf Merrett, 2004

The right of Wilf Merrett to be identified as the Author
of this work has been asserted in accordance with the
Copyrights, Designs and Patents Act 1988.

All rights reserved. No part of this book may be reprinted
or reproduced or utilised in any form or by any electronic,
mechanical or other means, now known or hereafter invented,
including photocopying and recording, or in any information
storage or retrieval system, without the permission in writing
from the Publishers.

British Library Cataloguing in Publication Data.
A catalogue record for this book is available from the British Library.

ISBN 0 7524 3307 5

Typesetting and origination by Tempus Publishing Limited.
Printed in Great Britain.

Contents

Acknowledgements

Some years ago members of Stroud Local History Society produced a plan of central Stroud showing the location of the various shops and businesses in the town in 1910, largely based on *Kelly's Directory* for that year. Using this information I embarked on a project to compare the Stroud shopping scene in 1910 with the post-war 1950s and the present day. As various material came to hand and memories were stirred this project expanded to include a potted history of each of the Stroud streets illustrated with sundry photographs and copies of old advertisements.

It was, however, mainly due to the generous co-operation of Annie Blick and Peckhams of Stroud in allowing me to use some of Edwin Peckham's excellent photographs that I had material worthy of publication. Additional photographs are by Albert Stanley Apperley © Stroud District (Cowle) Museum Trustees, The Museum in the Park, Stratford Park, Stroud, GL5 4AF, and further material is courtesy of Norman Andrews.

The following have been most helpful: Keith Apperley; Doreen Arnold; Howard Beard; David Burton; Percy Brownjohn; Bernard Dean; Brian Ward-Ellison; Gerald England; Jim Fern; Trevor Gallie; Eileen Halliday; Crystal Harrison; Margaret and Valerie Hodges; Ron Mace; Dennis and Muriel Mason; Mary Middleditch; Joan Pritchard; Les Pugh; Lionel Rutt; Eva Shipton; Joyce Shipton; Marion Tuck; Barbara Ward; Bill Yates and most of all my wife Betty who worked wonders with an often rebellious word processor.

Introduction

Before the nineteenth century, Stroud was a long, straggling small town with four main streets: High Street; King Street; Nelson Street and Silver Street, the main centres of activity being The Cross, The Shambles and the vicinity of the Royal George Hotel. The town gradually grew in importance as a centre for the surrounding villages and in 1824 the local poet and organist William Lawrence composed a lengthy poem *Stroudwater* extolling the virtues of Stroud referring to its 'handsome shops and inns' and 'the bustling throngs especially on market days'. Had Lawrence lived another eighty years his poetry might have been even more exuberant following the coming of the railway, new wider streets and impressive buildings like the Subscription Rooms and the Corn Hall. He would, however, have seen little change in the street pattern radiating from The Cross and several of the shops he patronised in 1824 still remained in the same families well into the twentieth century.

Stroud High Street in 1910 contained a diversity of shops including no less than six butchers and nine grocers. Other retailers included dyers, drapers, chemists, tobacconists, ironmongers, clothiers, newsagents, opticians etc. and this was typical of the rest of the town. In fact, local shops could supply every need and a visit to Gloucester or Cheltenham was an outing rather than a necessity. Housewives needed to purchase perishable goods two or three times a week, particularly in summer, with only a cool larder for storage. Items such as meat or fish were displayed openly without protection from dust and flies. On occasion, the whole frontage of the butcher's shop would be festooned with carcasses of lamb, pigs, poultry or game, possibly decorative but hardly hygenic. Presentation may not suit today's standards but the shop assistants, many of long standing, took a pride in their work and treated their customers with courtesy and efficiency. This conduct would have been instilled in them by the proprietors, mostly local men who often lived above or near their premises. They tended to be staunch members of the local Anglican or Nonconformist churches, active in civic affairs and generous supporters of the hospital and other local charities. Their anxiety to please their customers is evident by the somewhat obsequious advertments in the local press 'your kind patronage respectfully solicited' or 'in soliciting your favours we promise our best attention and most reasonable terms' and so on.

Most shops in 1910 were independent, but some multiple firms such as Liptons, Maypole, Home and Colonial (grocers) and Maynards (confectioners) were already established while Milwards and Stead and Simpsons competed with Revells, Stroud's main shoe retailer. There was a healthy rivalry and both independents and multiples coexisted for many years. Although the majority of shops were located in the town centre, it should be noted that Stroud contains no less than twenty thoroughfares designated as streets, and close inspection of the houses in Middle Street, Parliament Street and Lower Street will reveal some private properties still retaining their old shop frontages. These small shops including grocers, bakers, beerhouses and dressmakers must have produced little more than pocket money for the wife who probably looked after the premises while the husband worked elsewhere.

Mention should be made of the public houses, of which there was no shortage. Most were owned by the Stroud Brewery, their highest density being in the region of The Cross and the poorer quarters at the 'top of the town'. There were, altogether, some forty pubs in the town of which some thirty-five sold Stroud or Godsell's ale. Three of the best examples are: The Painswick; Greyhound and Green Dragon, all built to a high standard around 1900, but today only the Greyhound remains as a public house. The period between 1910 and 1940 saw considerable change with the erection of two new churches, two new cinemas, and the development of Stratford Park to provide a fine open air swimming pool and other amenities, and the building of new housing estates at Cashes Green and Summer Street. Woolworths moved from King Street to larger premises under the Victoria Rooms, Burtons erected a fine new shop to replace the run down Royal George Hotel, Stroud Co-operative Society built a departmental store on The Cross and Timothy Whites & Taylors erected a new shop in the High Street. Further development was obviously halted during the war years, but the town became even busier with the influx of large numbers of evacuees and war workers and the additional public transport required. Queues were to be seen everywhere, for food, buses, the cinema, and the influx of servicemen into the area including GIs meant that the pubs often ran dry.

Things slowly returned to normal after the war, but by now only three major independent grocers remained: The Cotswold Stores; Plesteds and Stranges. Several local butchers survived and while there were fewer tailors, milliners, music shops and china dealers, there were more cooked meat shops, dry cleaners, ladies hairdressers and shops selling prams and baby needs. In addition, Stroud now had a health stores, radio and electrical dealers and car accessory shops.

Soon things were to change dramatically following the demolition of large parts of upper Stroud and the building of more large estates at Paganhill, Cashes Green, Ebley and Rodborough. Stroud's first supermarket, Burtons, ousted The Green Dragon Inn to be itself replaced after a few years by Fine Fare and Keymarkets in the new Merrywalks shopping precinct. Being sited in the town centre, these stores attracted more shoppers into Stroud, but obviously had an adverse effect on the smaller shops unable to compete pricewise. The final blow came with the arrival of Tesco which soon meant the end of most of the remaining food shops. The International Stores which took over Withey & Withey in the 1920s moved to larger premises in Russell Street, but lacking parking facilities, closed down completely after a few years. The Cainscross and Ebley Co-op Society which had aquired Lewis and Godfrey's premises around 1960 eventually closed and its successor now trades as Oxford and Swindon Co-op from premises in Cainscross. Tesco was followed by Waitrose and Sainsburys and Great Mills opened a large DIY store just outside the town. These stores with their wide range of goods and convenient parking meant further closure of town shops and the new precincts of Cornhill and Merrywalks remained half empty. Convenience stores were replaced by charity shops, estate agents, travel agents, trendy clothes shops and the like. Men's outfitters all but disappeared and it became virtually impossible to buy furniture, kitchen appliances or electrical goods without visiting neighbouring towns.

Now at last there is an air of optimism. We have a fine new museum, a new cinema (albeit of controversial appearance) is in the offing, the Farmer's Market has proved a great success and the monthly decorative fair also held in the Cornhill market place ensures that this facility is well used. The Subscription Rooms has been refurbished as has the Cotswold Playhouse and the Space in Lansdown provides yet another entertainment venue. The Stroudwater Canal may be reopened within five years, including a marina in Stroud and eventual link with the Thames, providing a great boost for tourism. New housing developments close to the town centre such as the communal living scheme off Slad Road will hopefully increase footfall and induce more businesses (other than mobile phone vendors and internet cafés) into the town. Finally the sight of the newly refurbished Hill Paul building towering over the town seems like a beacon of hope for the future.

Wilf Merrett
May 2004

one

Old Stroud

The Cross

This small triangular open space created by the intersection of Tower Hill (Parliament Street), Nelson Street and High Street was the lively hub of old Stroud. The centrepiece was a cast iron lamp standard-cum-drinking fountain embellished with three metalic dolphins, which stood for a century before its destruction by an army vehicle during the war. A rescued dolphin may be seen in Stroud Museum.

At weekends market traders, cheapjacks and quacks erected their stalls, and crowds gathered to listen to their banter. Cure-all tonics were sold and painless dentistry practised, the general bustle and noise drowning the groans of the patients. The close proximity of three public houses, The Crown, King's Head and Corn Exchange ensured the presence of a few inebriates to the amusement or disgust of onlookers.

Before the arrival of the new Stroud Co-operative Society headquarters and departmental store in 1931, the site was occupied by several decrepit old shops including a dress shop somewhat presumptiously named Paris House. Several buildings were lost due to the construction of Cornhill, including Bradshaw's greengrocery premises and The Crown Inn. Bradshaws, established in 1874, were both wholesalers and retailers, and the florid lettering on their frontage proclaimed what additional merchandise was on offer. I recall that fruit and vegetables were displayed in profusion, potatoes etc., weighed on massive iron and brass scales and dates were cut from a huge block standing on the counter.

Franklin's boot and shoe shop nearby, established in 1868, lasted into the 1950s and another loss was the popular Cosy Corner Fish and Chip Restaurant, the first in Stroud to dispense with the use of newspaper. Arnold's, another chippy, was opposite just above Lewis's premises, and at the foot of Tower Hill (now Parliament Street) was Pitcher's antique shop, formerly occupied by 'Donkey' Wathern as a second-hand furniture store. This gentleman, a somewhat dour character with extremely long chin, manufactured his own special brand of furniture polish. For some years before demolition two of these houses were occupied by the local Spanish community consisting of hotel and restaurant waiters and their families and also a few old Republican refugees from Franco's regime in the 1930s.

Above: Most of the narrow pavement outside Bradshaw's greengrocery appears to be obstructed by baskets of produce, *c.* 1910.

Right: Merrett Bros photographers had a small studio at the Cross around 1885 before moving to Russell Street.

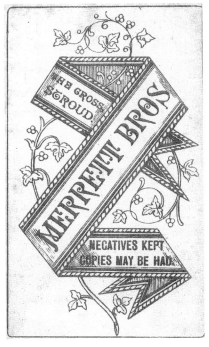

Above: The Cross *c.* 1920 with Philpott's carriers cart in the foreground.

Right: Phillpott's shoe repair shop occupying the former Paris House, *c.* 1920.

Opposite above: Townsfolk celebrating the opening of the Stroud Co-operative Society's new department store on The Cross, *c.* 1931.

Opposite below: The new store in all its glory. Note the old buildings on the left on the site of the present car park, *c.* 1938.

Above: Looking up Parliament Street from The Cross, with Arnold's Fish and Chip Restaurant, Hobbs carpet fitters and the tiny King's Head on the left, *c.* 1960.

Right: The Crown Inn was one of the few Cheltenham Brewery pubs in the town. Mr Walker, the licencee in the late 1930s, was blessed with four lively young daughters!

The Cross

No.	1910	1950	2003
35	R. Barrett chemist	J. Bartleman butcher	
36	Crown Hotel	Crown Hotel	*All demolished*
37	J. Bradshaw greengrocer	J. Bradshaw greengrocer	*in the 1970s*
38	Powles butcher	Day butcher	
39	Franklin footwear	Franklin footwear	
40	Clutterbuck glass/china Paris House Fashions	Stroud Co-op. Soc.	Silver Rooms Launderette
41	Wathern antiques	Pitcher antiques	
42	Kings Head Inn	Kings Head Inn	*All demolished*
43	Miss Williams tobacco	Tobacco Shop	*in the 1970s*
44	Lancaster cobbler	Arnold's fish fryers	
45	Corn Exchange Inn	Corn Exchange Inn	

Fish stalls on The Cross around 1910 watched by a host of flat-capped males.

Acre Street

This steep thoroughfare linking Middle Street with Parliament Street was once the location of a number of small businesses, as evidenced by the shop frontages still retained in several residential properties.

Although much of the street has been redeveloped in recent years, the most interesting building, the Salvation Army Citadel, remains. This unusual octagonal edifice built in 1763 originally served as a Wesleyan Chapel and John Wesley is said to have preached there each year prior to his death in 1791. The meeting room lower down the street dates from 1852 and is still used by the Open Brethren as a place of worship. Between these two buildings formerly stood two sizeable residences, Miss Knee's preparatory school occupying The Acre, while Baxter, a local builder, resided in Acre Hill House. A listed gazebo in the grounds of The Acre was unfortunately destroyed during the construction of the Wesley Flats that now occupy the site.

The Stroud Brewery was represented by The Butcher's Arms (now a private house) sited just above the Citadel, and by an off-licence on the corner of Chapel Street. Cheap accommodation was available at the Model Lodging House, an austere brick building presided over by Miss Reed. This amenity, together with several old cottages, was demolished to make way for the Chapel Street redevelopment.

Of the former two grocery shops at the bottom of the street, only one remains and R.B. Martin's business as fish, fruit, commissions salesman and herring curer has long since gone. H.A. Backhouse occupied No. 29 as hairdresser before moving to Middle Street and barber George Furley used the premises prior to his retirement, aged seventy-five, in 1986. Other pre-war businesses included greengrocers, booksellers, cobblers and dressmakers.

I recall one wizened old character living in the street who always dressed in the style of an old yeoman. He would have made a wonderful film extra and for a time his photograph was prominently displayed in Merrett's studio in Lansdown.

Opposite above: R.B. Martin and his young family pose outside his fruit and vegetable store on the corner of Chapel Street, *c.* 1900.

Above: The Salvation Army Citadel seen here around 1905. In recent years the roof has been lowered and the pointed arch fenestration removed.

Above: Acre Street Sunday School on 6 May 1935, King George V's Silver Jubilee Day. The children include Edna and Daisy Beckenham, Jimmy and Phyliss Hooper and Grace Hyam. The class leader Jesse Kibblewhite is standing on the right.

Left: The Butchers Arms seen here around 1910 is now a residential building. Following the removal of the cement rendering, the shape of the original small gabled cottage can now be clearly seen.

Opposite above: Little change at the lower end of the street. A number of private houses still retain the old shop fronts, *c.* 1970.

Opposite below: A coach negotiates the narrow street in this 1967 photograph. Soon afterwards all the property on the left was demolished for redevelopment.

Castle Street

Bearing right at the top of Nelson Street, one reaches this short street named after 'The Castle', an eighteenth-century mansion formerly the home of Paul Hawkins Fisher, author of *Notes and Recollections of Stroud*. The house, now divided into flats, bears no resemblance to a castle apart from the battlemented folly towers built into the garden wall.

Corbett House, separated from The Castle by an ancient cobbled thoroughfare, Castle Pitch, dates from the early nineteenth century. The prominent building situated at the start of the street is the former Blackboy School dating from 1840. Its name derives from the clock surmounted by the figure of a black boy who strikes the hours. This figure, resplendent in black and gold, was removed from shop premises demolished prior to the construction of Kendrick Street.

The nearby Infants' School built in 1903 is shortly to be enlarged to include juniors currently at Stroud Valley School. I attended this school from 1929 to 1931 during Miss Dearlove's long-lasting headship. This fine lady retired to London where she died in 1987 aged one hundred.

Between the schools stands the former Wesleyan Chapel built 1876 but closed some years ago due to serious structural problems. The building has since been renovated and converted into flats. The former congregation now worship jointly with the Anglicans at St Alban's Mission church in Parliament Street.

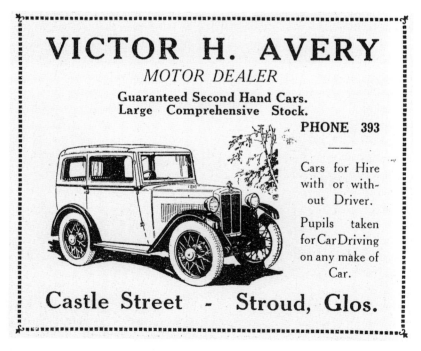

Above: A wide range of services advertised by this apparent 'one man' business, *c.* 1920.

Opposite above: A large noticeboard from around 1920 provides details of services at the Wesleyan Chapel, which has since been converted into flats.

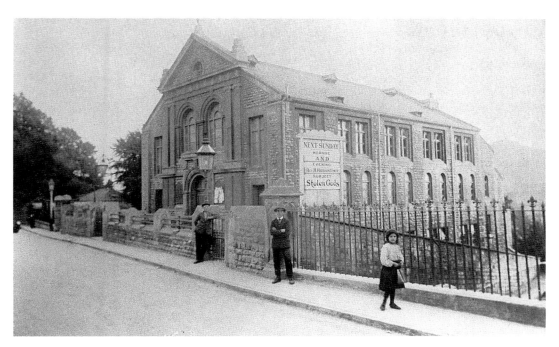

Above: A crowd of young scholars attracted by the photographer gather outside the Blackboy School around 1910.

Chapel Street

Chapel Street or Old Meeting Street, as it was formerly known, takes its name from the Old Chapel Congregational church, which was erected in 1705. The long driveway approach from Middle Street has recently been refurbished. Sadly, this old building needed considerable renovation and was demolished in 1977, but an attractive stained glass window was removed to Stroud Museum. The Sunday School building remains and is now used by the Pentecostal community.

One side of the street has been largely redeveloped as flats, but the old buildings opposite have been preserved and renovated, including a short pedimented terrace that once incorporated an off-licence. Surprisingly, the Stroud Co-operative Society once had its headquarters and departmental store in the street and this continued in use up to the 1950s.

A feature of the area, The Churs, are two narrow walkways connecting Chapel Street with Parliament Street and Middle Street. Bounded by high walls the sound of one's footsteps reverberated and children would stamp their feet to amplify the effect.

Following pedestrianisation the only vehicular access to the street is via Wood Street (opposite the Cotswold Playhouse). Once a densely populated area, no houses remain in this short thoroughfare.

Above: 1902 advertisement.

Right: The Old Chapel photographed shortly before demolition in 1977. Note the narrowness of the street.

Below: The galleried interior of the Old Congregational Chapel. Note the fine organ which was played by Sandy Macpherson in 1953.

Above: The original headquarters of the Stroud Co-operative Society occupied much of the right hand side of the street at a time when this was one of the most densely populated areas, *c.* 1910.

Left: William Barnes poses outside his off licence *c.* 1910.

Above: Demolition opposite has enhanced the aspect and outlook of the remaining houses in Chapel Street, as shown in this 1970 photograph.

Right: The Old Chapel, seen here around 1970, one of the 'ill favoured alleyways' referred to by Fisher, the local historian.

Church Street

Much of this old narrow street has disappeared following the construction of the Church Street car park. This involved the demolition of a row of attractive but neglected alms houses and a number of adjacent properties. Fortunately Rodney House (from around 1635), the former vicarage, remains and is now used as a nursing home. A post-war incumbent Revd Maltin said that he lived in a champagne house on a beer income.

The Bedford Arms on the corner of High Street, owned by the Stroud Brewery, and the Lamb Inn (now The Retreat Bistro), owned by Cheltenham Brewery, provided liquid sustenance while other pre-war businesses included: Lusty Plumber & Gas Fitter; Morris Cobbler; W.H. Pritchard Cabinet Maker and Upholsterer and a Mr Galey, whose sweet shop was opposite the church steps. This gentleman of strict religious persuasion would whisper that cigarettes hidden from view were available if required. A small brewery was sited almost opposite Rodney House and Henry Peglar, of Peglar's Cottage, was a local haulier.

Post-war businesses included David Keene's Veterinary Surgery, Trevor Gallie's Taxi and Coach Service, Audrey Butt's well patronised School of Dancing and more recently the Sunshine Health Stores, which continues to flourish.

Church Street Council School, now renamed Stroud Valley Junior School and once the province of the redoubtable Horace Doxsey, headmaster for nearly fifty years, is actually sited in Ryeleaze (formerly Belle Vue) Road. The site will shortly be redeveloped to provide residential accommodation.

The street's narrow outlet into the High Street has now been paved and pedestrianised and presents quite an attractive appearance. The car park has also recently been fully surfaced and provides visitors with a good impresion on arrival.

Opposite above: A baker's boy pauses by the old almshouses in this atmospheric view of old Stroud, *c.* 1930.

Opposite below: The High Street end of Church Street showing the entrance to the Bedford Arms shortly before its closure around 1967 with the Lamb Inn just beyond.

The ivy clad vicarage (now a nursing home) and the church remain. Everything else has gone for car parking, *c.* 1935.

Staff from Bells the drapers and friends about to embark on a trip aboard Trevor Gallie's coach, The Stroud Queen, around 1950. Shop owner Robin Elliott is in the centre of the photograph.

A view looking towards Uplands church. Part of Holloway's factory (with its 'tin' chimney) is seen on the right and has since been replaced by housing, *c.* 1970.

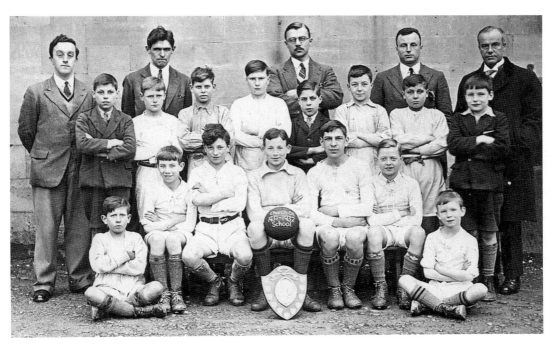

Staff and pupils at Church Street Council school in 1932. Teachers included here are, from left to right: Messrs Collinson; Mullins; Cox; Dean and headmaster Horace Doxsey.

Lower Street

Containing some of the oldest houses in the town and little changed over the centuries, this narrow street joins Castle Street at the junction with Spring Lane.

Residents at one time drew water from Hemlock Well (now considered unfit for drinking) and the large house at the corner of Spring Lane is appropiately called Hemlock Well House. An alleyway opposite led to Hollywell's scrap yard, and a few yards further up the street was Tuck's small shop and bakery, which lasted until the early 1950s. The converted flats opposite were, for nearly ninety years, occupied by England's second-hand furniture and antique business which closed in 1986.

A number of small businesses in the street included Critchley's confectionery shop, a general grocery store, a costumier and more recently Valley Confectionery sited near the approach to Piccadilly Mill. The mill was formerly the Sampson & Co. Ltd strap works, but has recently been divided up into a number of small industrial units.

The New Inn, the only public house in the street, closed some years ago to become a private residence. A previous landlord supplemented his income by operating a laundry in a large corrugated iron shed behind his premises. The Stroud Angling Club HQ was based at the New Inn.

A rather incongruous brick building opposite the New Inn was built following a serious fire that destroyed some of the oldest property in the street. Although it has the appearance of an Edwardian pub it has always been a private residence, and part of the original structure allegedly lies behind the brick façade.

Above: A 1960 view of this picturesque street. Unfortunately, demolition has left some gaps in the street.

Right: The gabled cottage on the left housed Tuck's bakery with its small shop projecting on to the pavement. The three ladies are believed to be members of the Tuck family who moved to Stroud from London early in the twentieth century, but had no connection with the Tucks at the Premier Café, *c.* 1910.

Below: The New Inn seen here around 1910 lacks the decorative art of the sign writer seen on so many contemporary Stroud pubs.

Middle Street

Running parallel with Lower Street at a slightly higher level, Middle Street, which still includes some interesting old properties, was much altered and 'improved' in Victorian times. A number of old cottages quite possibly damp and inconvenient were replaced by austere brick terraced houses; no doubt considered a big improvement by their new occupants. At the same time the roadway was built up to provide an even gradient resulting in some remaining cottages having downstairs rooms below street level.

Several residential properties still retain their old frontages providing evidence of retail trading, and in Victorian times businesses then operating included: bakers; butchers; grocers; wine and spirit merchants; coal merchants; wheelwrights; cobblers; tailors; auctioneers and furniture dealers. In more recent times the shops were mainly to be found at the lower end of the street and included Shore's the bakers, two grocers, a music shop and Backhouse's toy and novelty shop (nowadays a newsagents), much beloved by youngsters in pre-war days. Mr Backhouse, a short, dour character, operated as a barber in a back room, quite lacking in the jovial chat expected from those of similar calling. The music shop, sited in a charming little gabled house next to Backhouses, was the province of Mrs Trewern who always appeared through a beaded curtain whenever a loud bell announced the entry of a customer.

The Middle Street Garage has existed on the same site for many years still carrying out car repairs and MOTs, but it no longer serves petrol. Fragments of signwriting on an adjacent brick wall indicated that a dry-cleaning or laundry business formerly operated on the site. Further up the street stands the Old Bisley House (dating from around 1899) that replaced a much earlier inn of the same name and coexisted with the long defunct Sydney Arms. A small cul-de-sac opposite was the site of Sutton's nurseries, a popular venue for gardeners before the arrival of the huge garden centres.

The street ends at the former post office, becoming what is now known as Whitehall, and flanked on the upper side by rather imposing stone terraced residences, while at a lower level a line of old stone gabled cottages, now known as Piccadilly, border a track leading to a mill of that name.

Middle Street would have been familiar to John Wesley who regularly lodged there on his annual visits to Stroud, and the inventor John Canton spent his early years at a house in the street.

Entrepreneur Eric Peddle turned up in Stroud in the 1950s and set up a number of small businesses including the Willow Pattern Perfumery in George Street. The tea sets in this 1960 advert seem remarkably cheap!

The Backhouse family pose soberly outside their hardware and fancy goods shop with its comprehensive window display. Mr Backhouse was a prominent member of John Street Baptist church, *c.* 1920.

Backhouse's shop also appears in this later photograph. Mrs Trewern's music shop was in the old building with the steeply pitched roof, *c.* 1970.

The little girl in the foreground would be a centenarian if still alive, but this street looks much the same today as it was around 1910.

Whitehall, the 'posh' end of Middle Street photographed by Fred Major around 1920. He always encouraged passers-by to pose for his camera.

Nelson Street

This old street, severed from the High Street following the construction of Cornhill, still retains a number of interesting old buildings. The Stroud Co-operative building and Parliament Street car park combined to erase most of the old property on the north side of the street including some picturesque old seventeenth-century gabled cottages, which reputably had connections with General Wolfe. The south side of the street has fared better, although Godolphin House has been replaced by a modern building used by The Church of Latter Day Saints.

Passing the former Jo Jo's night club and adjacent fish and chip shop, the former Nelson Street post office (now a hairdressers)was at the corner of Farrs Lane. This rough trackway led to some pretty old cottages but passed a primitive slaughter house en route, which often supplied a form of entertainment to local youngsters.

Immediately above the lane, Joe's chippy occupies premises used for many years by my grandfather and two uncles as umbrella manufacturers. The remaining shops in the street included Wathern's furniture store Slades ladies wear, a couple of sweet shops and Mrs Dean's green-grocery store, outside which her son, suffering from sleeping sickness, would be found in a basketwork chair on sunny days. Both public houses, The Golden Fleece and Duke of York remain in use.

It is interesting to note that both Trafalgar House and Nelson House are to be found at the top of the street, and for a few years Nelson House was occupied by a family called Nelson.

FOR SMART
UP-TO-DATE
TAILORING

GO TO

W. J. SLADE

·18,
Nelson St.
STROUD

All Garments made on the premises by practical men.

—

Special Lines in
CAPS, SHIRTS,
HOSIERY, Etc.

Slade's tiny etablishment in Nelson Street was typical of many small businesses outside the town centre. This advertisement dates from 1902.

Above: During the 1920s Roger Quilter lived for several years with his grandfather in Merrett's umbrella shop currently occupied by Joe's Chippy. When he revisited Stroud over fifty years later he recalled the lively scene as bands and processions passed the shop. Shortly afterwards he produced this sketch in which he appears at an upstairs window, while his grandfather John Merrett stands in the doorway.

Left: The business lasted over a hundred years and this advertisement dates from around 1920.

Above: Few photographs have been found of this picturesque part of old Stroud, this pre-1920 postcard by Fred Major being an exception. The fine building in the middle distance is the old Corn Exchange demolished some forty years ago.

Right: Dean's humble grocery store at the top of the street must have been a boon to shoppers wishing to avoid the steep descent to the town centre, *c.* 1920.

Parliament Street

Present day Parliament Street stretches from The Cross at the top of High Street to Nouncells Cross, where it joins the Old Bisley Road. In living memory the lower steep stretch of the street was known as Tower Hill or Silver Street, but later renamed Hill Street after a respected lady councillor of that name. Nowadays nothing remains of the houses that flanked the old Tower Hill, and in their place we have the Stroud Police Station on one side and a car park opposite, dominated by the Wesley Flats. This development resulted in the loss of Tower House, Stroud's original reservoir,the Orange Tree Inn and Granny Ball's sweet shop and manufactory, apart from a number of interesting eighteenth- and nineteenth-century properties.

Just above the junction with Ryeleaze Road formerly stood The People's Hall, a simple non-denominational chapel erected by Opie Rodway, local draper and philanthropist, for the edification of the lower orders. Mr Rodway who lived in the secluded Tower House often arranged for the distribution of food to the local sick and needy. Opposite Ryleaze Close was the approach to Dyers Court, site of the original meeting place for Nonconformists, and my great - grandfather's first abode when he arrived in Stroud in the 1840s.

Apart from The Orange Tree Inn, the street was served by The Half Moon, The Star and higher up by The Butcher's Arms, Leopard, Cross Hands and the nearby Horse and Groom. All of these inns, apart from The Cross Hands, have been either demolished or converted to residential use. The same applies to the small shops and businesses, but Osborne's long-established Marine Stores, really a scrapyard, still survives as a pioneer of modern day recycling.

St Alban's Mission church, now used jointly by Anglicans and Methodists, is built on the site of Stroud's original workhouse. Close by is the former Primitive Methodist chapel which has now been greatly extended and converted to become a small theatre known as The Cotswold Playhouse. Almost opposite, the former Parliament Street School (since resited in Old Bisley Road), now serves as the local registration office, providing excellent facilities for civil weddings.

Opposite above: The lower end of the street was once better known as Tower Hill. Alan and Joan Tucker's bookshop on the left was previously the famed sweet shop and manufactory of Granny Ball's, *c.* 1965.

Opposite below: On a warm sunny day a mother and her daughter plod wearily up the hill with a heavy load of shopping, *c.* 1965.

Above left: The Orange Tree, one of a number of pubs in the street that may have lost its licence or been demolished.

Above right: Parliament Street seen here looking towards High Street. All the property on the right has been demolished to make way for the police station and magistrates' court, *c.* 1965.

Above: Higher up the street Osborne's scrapyard is seen on the right just above the People's Hall, last used as a Pentecostal church, *c.* 1960.

Right: All the property opposite St Alban's church has been replaced by uniform modern housing, *c.* 1960.

Left: Jack Gregory and Phyliss Brownjohn photographed after their wedding at St Alban's church. The sign for the Butchers Arms can be seen on the right, *c.* 1940.

Below: The Primitive Methodist Chapel built in 1863, has since been extensively altered and enlarged to serve as the Cotswold Playhouse, *c.* 1920.

Summer Street

Once known as Somer Street, this is hardly a street in the true meaning of the word. Stretching for half a mile past stone terraces, bungalows and council houses, it eventually joins the rural Slad Lane. Currently served by one grocery store, there were other small businesses within living memory including The Oddfellows Arms, no longer identifiable following the removal of its three ornamental bays.

The town end of the street is dominated by the Nouncells Cross flats which command far-reaching views towards the Severn, and almost opposite some of the allotment holders have erected quite elaborate sheds–cum–summerhouses to provide a break from their exertions.

A rare photograph of Summer Street from around 1908. The lad is sitting on a very substantial wall, part of which still remains above the allotments.

Left: The Oddfellows Arms, around 1910, formed part of the terraced row of cottages shown in the preceding photograph, but is nowadays indistinguishable from the adjacent houses.

Below: No doubt the Summer Street police station (seen here around 1970) was a very necessary adjunct, as the main Stroud police station at Beeches Green was nearly a mile away. This building was removed for road widening some thirty years ago.

two

Four Main Streets

George Street

George Street was, like King Street, named in honour of George III's fleeting visit to the town in 1788. Better planned and with more uniform architecture than the older streets, George Street is now largely occupied by banks, building societies, estate agents and charity shops.

The principal shop fifty years ago was probably Clark's Drapers (formerly Redfern) which claimed to be the 'shopping centre of Mid Gloucestershire'. It later became a branch of McKilroy's and is now a video shop. John Clark, the owner, was a genial character who like so many of his business contemporaries was involved in local activities, his main interest being the Cotswold Players. He would have been in competition with Johnson's Ladies' and Gent's Outfitters just across the street. Established at the turn of the nineteenth century Johnson's was taken over by the enterprising Mr N.F.W. Gibson shortly after the Second World War. This gentleman, an active local councillor, was regarded as a firm but fair employer who expected a high standard from his staff. Joyce Shipton, who worked at his previous shop in 1939, received 2s 6d per week with the prospect of an additional 2s 6d every six months.

The Midland Bank (now HSBC) occupies the site of Park's General and Furnishing Drapery shop. Sidney Park generously donated the area of land off Slad Road known as Park Gardens to the town as a memorial to his son who was killed during the First World War

The recently vacated shop at No. 4 was formerly a pharmacy. The proprietor, Mr H.H. North, installed the distinctive curved windows, but these were not appreciated by Mr Whiteoak, his successor, as they restricted his display. Fortunately the proposal to remove the windows was vetoed by the local council on the grounds that they were a distinctive feature adding character to the street.

Walkers Stores 'Pioneers of Popular Prices', now occupied by Manns the jewellers, was the scene of a pre-war tragedy, when coping stones damaged by frost fell and killed two pedestrians.

The former Gas Company showroom, which was next door at No. 7, is now a charity shop and for many years the upstairs was used as a photographic studio by my father Mark Merrett who also had a small studio at the top of Russell Street. More recently Ruby Harper, the hairdresser and well-known singer, occupied the upper floor.

Another long-established hairdresser was Madame Sawyer (now the Bristol and West Building Society). Pretty young apprentices would often be seen gazing idly at the passers by. I was surprised to learn, not only that a schoolmaster friend patronised this establishment, but also that the proprietor was in fact male.

Two little shops squeezed tightly together were occupied by Poole the optician and the Sunshine Health Stores. The proprietor of the latter was a Miss Woolf, followed after a few years by Lil Smith, both from Whiteway Colony. The shop sold herbal remedies and Prothero bread, and always seemed to be offering kittens for adoption. Hidden away at the back of the shop was a small private area that acted as a convenient waiting room for colonists and friends before they caught the bus home.

C. and A. Whitehall at No. 23 (now Western Carpet Fitters) specialised in cooked meat products and were noted for their high quality meat paste sold in small ceramic pots sealed with solidified fat, sadly no longer available. I recall that the assistants were predominently male and some may have spent all their working life with same employer.

In pre-war days shops changed hands infrequently and other long-established concerns no longer with us include: Redmans Tailors and Outfitters; Humpidge Seedsman and Florist; the Singer Sewing Machine Co.; Western National Bus Office; Hills and Scotts jewellers; Burr's music shop; the Stroud Creamery and Walters popular cake shop. The only public house in the street was the Post Office Inn, which has now become Sawyers Estate Agency.

Buildings such as the Kendrick Hall reflect the growing importance of Stroud as a shopping and administrative centre in the late Victorian era. Incidentally all the cars in this 1963 photograph are British!

Set back from the street is the Stroud Subscription Rooms dating from 1833, centre for balls, musical events and more recently brass band festivals. The small piazza fronting the rooms has recently had its second makeover in thirty years, not to everyone's taste, however, the building, together with the Congregational church to the left and the Kendrick Street former Cloth Hall to the right, forms quite an impressive townscape. The area in front of the rooms was originally grassed with trees and shrubs enclosed by railings within which stood two Russian cannons, relics of the Crimean War. Both cannons and railings went for scrap during the war, temporarily replaced by a large brick air raid shelter. The Rooms were referred to as the Stroud Valley Community Centre, providing refreshment and entertainment mainly for young people during, and for several years after, the war.

The short length of George Street opposite Sim's clock includes Bateman's long-established sports shop, which originally sold tobacco, toys, guns and clothing as well as sports equipment. Ferris and Woodward next door were excellent gents outfitters and the Stroud News premises were on the corner of John Street. A popular café, The Flamingo, formerly in Gloucester Street, occupied rooms high up in the building approached by a somewhat temperamental lift, but the view was worth it.

Left: The Post Office Inn, around 1910, which could be accessed from George Street and Russell Street, closed some forty years ago. The premises are now occupied by Sawyers Estate Agents.

Below: No expense was spared when the County Agricultural Show was held at Stroud in 1907. The main streets were festooned with flags and bunting, and triumphal arches erected, some of which were later reused in other locations including Cirencester.

Opposite above: At election times crowds gathered outside the Subscription Rooms for the declaration of the poll. Nowadays we are content to hear the results on TV or radio.

Opposite below: A sombre wartime view. The small ornamental garden and Russian cannons have been replaced by an unsightly air-raid shelter that was fortunately never required, *c.* 1940. Note the proliferation of direction signs and the Ritz poster advertising the film *Jamie*.

50

Above and right: Redmans gents outfitters following a makeover around 1930 and the same shop as it appeared in a 1902 advertisement. George Redman, a pillar of the local Baptist church, was the father of Roderick who ultimately became Professor of astrophysics at Cambridge and President of the Royal Astronomical Society. This shop, like Gibsons, has since been absorbed by the enlarged HSBC bank.

Opposite above: An Edmunds & Humpidge van is seen parked outside their George Street premises. Like similar shops, advice on horticultural matters was readily available, something often lacking at our large garden centres today.

Opposite below: A good humoured wartime bread queue outside Walters' premises. It must have taken hours to serve all these customers. Note the huge pair of spectacles suspended over the premises of Poole the optician.

GEO. REDMAN & SON,

Tailors, Clothiers,
Outfitters,
Shirtmakers and Hosiers.

27, GEORGE STREET,
STROUD.

TAILORS.	We are PRACTICAL TAILORS. All work cut on the premises, and made by experienced workmen. Style and Fit guaranteed.
CLOTHIERS.	A large and well-assorted stock of Men's and Boys' Suits, Trousers, Overcoats, etc. Private Showrooms for fitting on.
OUTFITTERS.	GENTS' OUTFITTING of every description. Best Value at Popular Prices.
SHIRTMAKERS.	SPÉCIALITÉ: OUR OWN MAKE SHIRTS. Made in Oxford, Regatta, Drill, Flannelette, etc.
HOSIERS.	All the best makes of GENTS' HOSIERY kept in stock. PANTS and VESTS in every material and weight.

GEO. REDMAN & SON, 27, George Street, Stroud.
38

CORNER OF KING ST. AND GEORGE ST. STROUD

Above: Ruby Harper's smart hairdressing salon around 1950. Ruby, furthest from the camera, was not only a first-class hairdresser, but also a well-known contralto singer. Much in demand as a soloist, she was a member of the Stroud Light Music Choir, the Painswick Operatic Society and also the Gloucester Operatic and Dramatic Society.

Opposite above: Mr N.F.W. Gibson, having aquired Johnson's drapery business, erected this impressive shop front contrasting with the tiny premises occupied by the Sunshine Health Stores next door, *c.* 1950.

Opposite below: Clark's (formerly Redston's) extensive premises operated on three floors including the basement. John Clark, the proprietor, was a well-known member of the Cotswold Players, *c.* 1920.

George Street

No.	1910	1950	2003
1&2	Redfern draper	Clark draper	Blockbuster video
3	Cox tailor	Winfield seedsman	Stroud Video Centre
4	Bryant antique furniture	H. North chemist	*vacant*
5	Barnard pianos	Collins stationer	Mr Minit shoe repairs
6	Luscombe sadler	Stroud Gaslight	Sue Ryder
7	Hooper cycle agent	& Coke Co.	charity shop
8	Walkers Stores	Walkers Stores	Mann jeweller
8a		West Nat. bus office	
9	Singer Sewing Co.	Singer Sewing Co.	Age Concern
			charity shop
10	Horwood fancy goods	J. Fitzwater elect.	Parker estate agent
11,12 13	Subscription Rooms	,,	,,
14	Washbourne milliner	*demolished*	*demolished*
15	Hill watchmaker	Hill watchmaker	Crumbs sandwich bar
16	Ludgate saddler	Stroud Creamery	Centurion Vintners
17	Post Office Inn	Post Office Inn	Sawyers estate agent
18&19	Wilts & Dorset Bank	National Provincial Bank	NatWest Bank
20	Okey bootmaker	Madame Sawyer hairdresser	Bristol & West
			Building Society
21	Butcher milliner	Walter's cake shop	R.A. Bennett
			estate agent
22	Burton watchmaker	F.C. Scott watchmaker	Heritage
23	J. White printer	Whitehall's cooked meats	Western Carpets
24	Hobbs confectioner	Poole optician/Sunshine	Poole optician
		health store	
25&26	Johnson draper	N.Gibson draper	HSBC Bank
27	Redman outfitter	F.G. Hawkins outfitter/	,,
		Westminster bank	
28	Park draper	Midland Bank	,,
29	Holloways	Bateman's Sports	
30	Cloth Hall	Ferris & Woodward	Bateman's Sports
31		Ice cream parlour	Four Clocks antiques
32	Stroud News Office	Stroud News Office	Touché (ethnic)
			,,

High Street

Like so many High Streets this is the busiest and longest shopping street in the town, also the steepest and most irregular in width and variety of architecture. Sadly this irregularity also extends to the the block paving introduced following pedestrianisation, which can prove hazardous for the unwary.

Some years ago there were plans to bulldoze much of the Lower High Street to create an open space linking up with Bank Gardens. Later a modified plan was thwarted by determined protestors who occupied the threatened rooftops, effectively preventing demolition. Some rebuilding has however taken place in traditional style, although this cannot be said for the architecture and material used in the construction of the Lloyds TSB Bank.

The early eighteenth-century bank house at the bottom of the street, now The Lansdown Clinic and previously the Stroud UDC offices, was owned by the Winterbotham family who in 1930 generously donated their gardens to the town as a public amenity.

The present Bon Marché occupies the site of Revell & Sons Ltd boot and shoe retailers, for many years the largest footwear shop in the town with a branch in Bath. I believe it was the first local shop to install an X-ray machine as a fitting aid, now an illegal item.

Before the advent of the supermarkets a quarter of the seventy shops in the street were food shops, grocers, butchers or bakers. The multiples were well represented by Liptons, George Mason, Star, Home & Colonial, International, Hunters and Maypole. All of these shops were of a stereotyped design offering high standards of hygiene using much decorative tiling and marble with goods attractively presented. Eva Shipton, who spent several wartime years at the Maypole, recalls the regular inspections and strict cleanliness and efficiency demanded. The Stroud shop employed a manager, two assistants and a lad. For much of the time, the manager was busy behind the scenes but would always appear to deal with an important or difficult customer. It was fascinating to watch the assistants operating the bacon slicer, patting the butter into shape and packaging the goods in brown paper tied with string.

Withey & Withey, Stroud's principal grocers, were wine and spirit merchants since 1806 and were succeeded some 120 years later by the International Tea Stores who subsequently moved to larger premises in Russell Street. Moonflower now occupies No. 52 in succession to Handiland.

Another grocer, William Thomas Sims, whose shop has been replaced by Lloyds TSB, was responsible for the fine memorial clock that bears his name. He not only provided the money for the clock but also set up a trust fund to provide Christmas dinners for the poor.

Butchers included Eastmans, London Central Meat Co., Seabrook & Hughes, Bainbridges, Warners and Pritchards (now Imprint), whose small primitive slaughter house was just behind the shop. The only fishmonger in the High Street prior to MacFisheries was 'Fishy' Lee of Central Fish Supply who also festooned his shop front with poultry at Christmas time. Cooked meat products were sold by three good local firms, Bathes, Chapmans and Hilliers.

S. & R. Ball, and later Theyers, were the main greengrocers and Jimmy Ball, parading outside his premises, would harrangue the prospective customers while his hard-working wife and daughter served within.

The brothers Clissold, one sporting a fiercely waxed moustache, had a small bakery near the Cross. Their popularity increased at weekends when large bags of unsold bread and buns could be acquired for a few pence.

Until recently Maynards and Barsby's sold sweets and chocolates, but pre-war Mrs Lucas (whose shop is now Woodruffs) stocked a variety of gobstoppers, sherbet fountains and licorice delights to entice youngsters.

Smith & Lee, the long-established ironmongers, whose closure is a great loss to the town, occupied one of the oldest buildings, outside which a florist can be found at weekends. Sadly No. 5, opposite, no longer displays its decorative rooftop urns, but the pretty venetian window over the former Milwards shop remains. Lower down, the bland plastic fascia of Thomas Cook's effectively obliterates the mullion windows of the once attractive gabled building it occupies. This criticism applies to so many shops whose garish prefabricated name boards destroy the ambiance and individuality of buildings and streets.

The arrival of a new retailer always created much interest. Such was the case when Timothy Whites and Taylors opened their branch in a brand new building around 1935 (now Bewise). Their pharmacy would have competed with Smiths and Coleys higher up the street, but this newcomer also sold kitchenware and other domestic requirements. At about the same time Burtons the tailors, sporting neon lighting, opened at No. 12 just above Bedford Street before moving to more prestigious premises in King Street shortly before the war.

Long before Burtons, Smiths of Alma House (established shortly after the Crimean War) were the town's principal gents outfitters. Whitchers continued and expanded the business, but New Look now occupies the premises. Dixons replaced Bells, drapers in Stroud for a hundred years, and noted for the overhead cableway running between assistants and cashier. Other well-known firms no longer with us include: Mitchells, another drapers; Walter Collins the stationers, later Marriots; JT Davis basket and rope retailers and Marsh the optician.

In those far-off days Stroud and the High Street in particular could supply almost every household need.

Pritchard's advertisement from around 1950.

Much patriotic fervour evident in this photograph of the High Street decorated for the 1907 County Agricultural Show.

The same location a few years later. Withey & Withey have a new shop frontage, and a delivery van belonging to a competitor, Mills Bros, stands outside, *c.* 1910.

Above: A sombre view of Hillier's premises on the corner of Kendrick Street from around 1920.

Above: The Council Chambers decorated for the Silver Jubilee (of George V and Queen Mary) in 1935.

Right: Charles Hall, licencee of the Bedford Arms, pictured outside the pub on the corner of Church Street, *c.* 1910.

Opposite below: George Mason, part of a large grocery chain of shops that no longer exists. During the early 1950s the premises were occupied by the Star Supply Stores, presumably replaced by Mason's some years later, *c.* 1960.

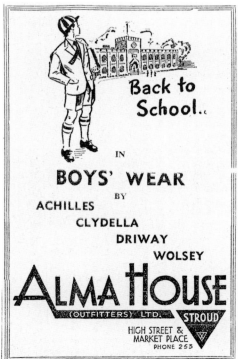

Above: The name and date on this building indicates that it was built during or just after the Crimean War. Stroud's largest gent's outfitters (seen here around 1950), it traded as Smith & Son for many years before its aquisition by Whitchers in 1964. During David Burton's seventeen years as manager, the business continued to prosper, but like Stroud's other remaining outfitters eventually closed around 1990. The premises are now occupied by New Look (ladies fashions).

Left: A 1957 Advertisement for Alma House.

Above: Currys put on a fine display in 1935 when a new bicycle cost less than £4. The models on show would need to be securely padlocked today.

Right: No. 6 was one of the oldest buildings in the High Street seen here, *c.* 1960. Foster's fascia has obliterated a pretty three-paned mullion window.

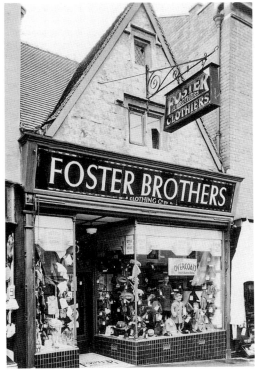

WHOLESALE
FRUIT & POTATO
MERCHANTS.

DEALERS IN
ALL KINDS OF
ENGLISH & FOREIGN
FRUITS.

DIRECT
IMPORTERS

WHEN
IN
SEASON

FRUITERERS   S & R. BELL   GREENGROCERS

Above: Two butchers and part of Darrell Chapman's excellent cooked meat shop, *c.* 1960. Baimbridges, the last remaining butchers in Stroud, closed two or three years ago. The Slippery Nipple boutique now operates here.

Right: Henry Llewellyn's carcass display would hardly meet today's hygienic regulations, *c.* 1920. The premises later became The Central Fish Supply Co., and more recently Wash Vac, but are shortly to be converted into flats.

Opposite: The premises of S. & R. Ball following post-war modernisation, *c.* 1960. The shop had no counter but usually there were several assistants at hand to ensure an efficient service.

'Fishy' Lee of Central Fish Supply in the guise of poulterer, probably in the late 1930s. One hopes the weather was cool and that he had plenty of customers!

A splendid example of the signwriter's craft, *c*. 1936. The shopkeeper, Mr Coombes, ran the business for only a few years prior to the Second World War when Pritchards next door were selling sausages for 8d per pound.

Above left: This 1937 display by Timothy Whites was intended to counteract the adverse publicity concerning the use of aluminium utensils in cooking.

Above right: Staff of Mitchells the drapers in the late 1940s, including Muriel Hogg, Jean Clarke, Olive and Margaret Osborne and Janet Hopkins. Muriel Mason (née Hogg) recalls having to sweep the pavement and clean the windows first thing in the morning. She worked a six day week with Thursday afternoons free.

Opposite: Timothy Whites built this fine new shop in the mid–1930s, and Peckham has even included some window-shoppers in the photograph. The premises are now occupied by Bewise.

Above: MacFisheries shop on the corner of Bedford Street was most efficiently managed by a Mr Cook, *c.* 1960. Ice was sprinkled amongst the fish to keep it cool.

Left: A neat display in this small modern butcher's shop sited next to Pritchard's for some thirty post-war years, *c.* 1960.

High Street

No.	1910	1950	2003
1	Mayo milliner	Baker's footwear	Andrews estate agent
2	Coward tailor	Kirby cooked meats	High Street Chippy
3a	Wright tobacconist	Wright tobacconist	Phoenix Rising
3b	Johnson's dyers	Johnson's dyers	,,
4	Hawkins grocer	Timothy Whites chemist	Bewise clothes
5	Park draper	Star Supply Stores	Clarke footwear
		Phillips shoes	C&G Building Society
6	Reynolds tailor	Foster Bros clothiers	Thomas Cook travel
7	Heslop leathergoods	Hepworths clothiers	Forbuoys newsagents
8	Eastman butcher	Dewhursts butchers	,,
9	Heslop carrier	Marsh optician	Boots optician
10	Maynard sweet shop	Maynard's sweet shop	,,
11	White chemist	Mitchells draper	Pound Shop
12	White Lion Inn	Mac Fisheries	Quicksilver Arcade
13	Aldridge china/glass	LCM Butchers	Moonflower 2
14	Clutterbuck furniture	Curry elect.	Pennyfarthing Café
15	Smith & Lee ironmongers	Smith & Lee ironmongers	*Vacant*
16	Hillier bacon curers	Lennards shoes	Help the Aged charity shop
17	Horder draper	Theyers greengrocer	Millets
20	,,	,,	,,
21	Davis rope /twine	Davis rope/twine	*Vacant*
22	Laidlaw baker	Hunters tea stores	Klick Photos
23	Cotswold Stores grocery	S. & R. Ball greengrocers	Stroud bookshop
24	Star Tea Co grocers	A.G.Andrews elect.	Organic Café
25	Mrs Bower coffee tavern	Bainbridge butcher	Slippery Nipple fashions
26	Nelson butcher	Clarke Bros elect	Lowes picture framer
27	Llewellyn fishmonger	Lee fishmonger	Wash Vac elect.
28	Gabb butcher	Parsons butcher	Just Hair barbers
29	Lee newsagent	Cotswold Cleaners	Young florist
30	Stevens saddler	Exchange & Mart	Eclipse
31	Misses Wynn pawnbroker	Pritchard butcher	Inprint
32	Spray pawnbroker	Seabrook & Hughes butcher	Via Sacra
33	Walter Guilding confectioner	Clissold confectioner	Bishopston Trading
34	E. Garrett café	Cosy Comer fish & chips	Citizen's Advice Bureau

Nos 35 to 44 demolished (see Cross)

No.	1910	1950	2003
45	Eastman butcher	R. Lewis elect.	Connexions
46	Howell gas fitter	D. Barsby sweet shop	Sprauney antiques
47	Nelson Inn	Stroud Repair Company	Heart Foundation

48	Tyler furniture	Rite Wools	Internet Café
49	White& Pratten costumiers	Marriott newsagent	Antics model shop
50	Stroud Co-operative Society	Bedford Arms Inn	Breadhead
51	Bedford Arms Inn	Bedford Arms Inn	Sahara ethnic goods
52	Owen printer/stationer	Zachary wines and spirits	New Look
53	Smith outfitters	Smith outfitters	New Look
54	Smith chemist	Smith chemist	Pure Clothes
55	Withey & Withey grocers	International Stores	Moonflower
56	Bell & Co drapers	Bell & Co drapers	Dixons elect.
57	Coley chemist	Coley chemist	Boots chemist
58	Mills Bros grocers	Millwards footwear	”
59	George Mason	Clarke Bros elect.	Special Occasions
60	Maypole Dairy Co.	Maypole Dairy Co.	Dorothy Perkins
61	Stead & Simpson footwear	Wallpaper Stores	Going Places
62	Home & Colonial grocers	Home & Colonial grocers	”
63	Hughes tobacconist	Hughes tobacconist	”
64	Hilton footwear	Iles leather items	”
65	Lipton grocers	Lipton grocers	
66 & 67	Revell's Shoes	Revell's Shoes	Bon Marché
	”	”	”
	Bank House	SUDC Offices	Done bookmaker
	Residential	SUDC Offices	Lansdown Clinic

Kendrick Street

This, the newest of the main shopping streets in the town, dates from 1872. Several buildings in the High Street were demolished to create this new thoroughfare,which passed through Kendricks's Orchard to join George Street. The east side of the street wass lined by two blocks of property, a brick terracotta-faced terrace of shops adjoining the High Street and a line of stone buildings adjacent to and complementing the former Cloth Hall in George Street. This latter section incorporated the Kendrick Hall which has had a variety of uses over the years including a café, lecture rooms and as a part of the Technical College.

The brick terrace contained about eight shop units, the principal occupant for many years being Fawkes Stores, grocers, wine and spirit merchants, providing stiff competition for Withey & Withey nearby. In 1923, the Cotswold Stores acquired Fawkes's business having rapidly expanded from small beginings in Painswick. This company had twenty branches in the south Cotswolds, a bacon factory in Nympsfield and headquarters at Far Hill. Unfortunately like all other town grocers, the Cotswold Stores could not compete with the new supermarkets and finally closed some thirty years ago.

Stroud was well supplied with shoe shops and two of these, Lennards and Olivers, faced each other across Kendrick Street. As a young lad Ron Mace was employed by Olivers for a pittance and five days annual leave, one of his duties being to care for the manager's prize rabbits. There was fierce rivalry between the two shops, both displaying cheap shoes suspended on poles outside their premises. During quiet periods the staff were instructed to constantly remove and replace shoes from this display, to give the impression that trade was brisk even when the shop was empty. Staff were also warned never to let a customer leave without making a purchase, if only a shilling pair of stockings! The pretty young assistants at Lennards were similarly instructed to look busy and entertained Ron and his collegues by teetering to and from their display in three-inch stilettos.

The premises on the corner of Threadneedle Street has been a bakery for generations, remembered by older residents as Fowlers (now Walkers) it still retains its Victorian frontage unlike the remainder of the shops in the street. For some years after the Second World War flour was still delivered to the bakery by Workmans of Cam using Sentinel steam lorries. The manageress, Miss Mayo, regarded as something of a martinet by the staff, was well disposed to polite youngsters, and as a child I usually emerged clutching some free sugary confection.

Smith's Leather and Fancy Goods shop opposite, occupies premises which in around 1930 replaced a rather ornamental single storey structure that served as Thomas Cratchley's Glass and China Emporium, offering the largest and cheapest stock in the 'Borough' of Stroud. This redevelopment took place when the ambitious Mr Sanderson came to the town requiring a modern building with extensive glass frontage to display his frocks,coats, costumes and furs, for which purpose Cratchley's Emporium was inadequate. After some years Blinkhorns of Gloucester used the shop for the sale of furniture, carpets, curtains and electrical goods. Mr Smith, the present owner, acquired the premises in 1966.

Mr Sanderson also turned his attention to the Old Cloth Hall where new shop frontages were inserted. He suggested in his brochure that the town particularly needed an exclusive hatter, a multiple tailor and a high class café complete with orchestra. How we could do with someone with his drive and ambition today! Since 1930 this corner unit has been occupied by Bateman's Sports Shop, while adjacent premises formerly included Brown's Café and the Wessex Library. Davis Champion and Payne's rather drab premises were a little higher up the street, so unlike the colourful presentation seen in estate agent's windows nowadays.

Opposite Walker's a corner doorway provided access to the offices of the Natioinal Assistance Board and the Inland Revenue PAYE department. The steep stairway must have been a serious deterrent to the less able applicants!

Vivian Taylor's elegant ladies' dress shop pictured when it opened in the 1930s.

One of Mr Sanderson's photographs publicising Kendrick Street. Walkers (then Fowlers) bakers on the corner looks exactly the same today! Firms in this street included Lennards, Eastmans, Olivers, Sandersons and Cotswold Stores Ltd.

Another Sanderson photograph showing his own premises after redevelopment in the 1920s. The caption reads: 'One of the best developments of the town occurred when Mr Sanderson purchased a block of property in Kendrick Street, pulled it down and erected this up-to-date shop which was opened about two years ago. The interior is beautifully arranged with large showrooms and fitting rooms, and there is also a fine central gallery. The fittings and staircase are of fine Austrian oak and the ground floor showrooms have a fine parquet flooring and real Persian rugs.'

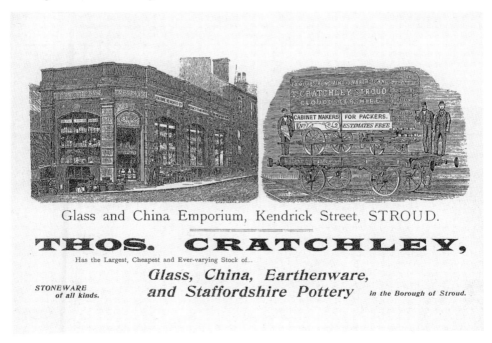

The same location is seen in this 1902 advertisement. Note the reference to the Borough of Stroud.

A general view of lower Kendrick Street showing names that are now only memories, *c.* 1960. Wilkes household furnishers were constantly moving, originally in King Street Parade and later London Road.

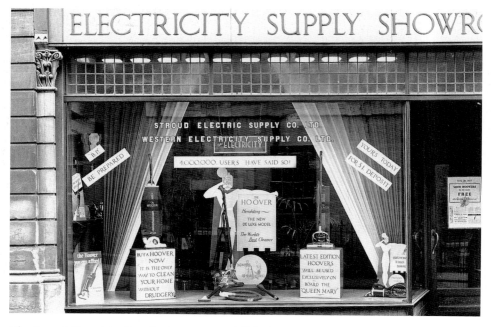

The Stroud Electricity Supply showroom *c.* 1935. Later as M.E.B they relocated to the High Street but now have no presence in the town.

The Cotswold Stores (formerly Fawkes' Stores) were considered to be upmarket, while Pankhurst's like Pompadours in King Street were the 'in' places for hairdressing. The neat shop frontages are in keeping with the architectural style of the building, *c.* 1950.

GIBSONS FOR ALL KINDS OF DRAPERY

SPECIALISTS IN

**HOSIERY
UNDERWEAR
FANCY GOODS
DRESSES AND
MILLINERY**

*We Sell Gibsons and
Ballito Hose. Pure
Silk 1/6½ and 2/- pair*

16-18, Kendrick Street
STROUD

Branch at
**71, Cricklade Street
Cirencester**

Above: A display of blankets does little to improve the rather drab appearance of Gibson's drapery, *c.* 1938. His later premises in George Street were a considerable improvement.

Left: The elegant young lady featured in Gibson's advertisements for many years.

Kendrick Street

No.	1910	1950	2003
1	Thomas Cratchley china and glass	Blinkhorns furnishers	Smiths leather goods and petshop
2	Thomas Cratchley china and glass	Blinkhorns furnishers	Smiths leather goods and petshop
3	Lennards	Hilliers/ Barbsy	KNP clothing
4	Hillier's bacon curers	Lennards' shoes	Help the Aged
5	Horder draper	Scotch Wool Shop	Millet
6	Oliver's footwear	Olivers footwear	Far Fetched
7	Eastman butcher	Eastman butcher	Lunn Poly travel
8	Fawkes' Stores	Cotswold Stores	YMCA charity shop
9	,,	,,	Cotswold Care
10	Fletcher butcher	Pankhurst hairdresser	Kodak Express
11	Fowler confectioner	Fowler confectioner	Walkers bakers
12	Holloway Bros offices	Govt. Offices	Summerbees hairdressers
13	,,	Wilkes furnisher	Made in Stroud
14	Stroud Water Co.	Limbrick optician	,,
15	WR parcel depot	Electricity Supply show room	Kanes Video
16	Davis Champion & Payne	Davis Champion & Payne estate agents	Halifax Building Society
17	MR parcel depot	,,	,,
18	Holloway Bros offices	Wessex Library	Brookes cleaners
19	,,	Brown's Café	KNP clothing
20	,,	Bateman's Sports	Bateman's Sports

King Street

One of the few level streets in Stroud, King Street has benefitted from its recent pedestrianisation. Together with the wider King Street Parade it offers shopkeepers some of the prime positions in the town. Most existing businesses are recent arrivals other than the three banks, but WH Smith's small shop has remained at No. 15 for over a century. Woolworth's have also been in Stroud for many years, moving from King Street to larger premises in Kings Street Parade in the 1930s. Here they initially occupied most of the ground floor of the Victoria Rooms, a large public building dating from 1831, but some forty years ago the store was expanded to provide retail services on two floors served by an escalator, and only a small section of the original building remains over the shoe shop.

Among the old firms that have disappeared is the grocery shop of S.M. Strange, one of the last to admit defeat following the advent of the supermarkets. The firm specialised in bananas, and following a delivery an assistant was shocked to find a huge spider, probably a tarantula, among the fruit. The assistants were predominantly male, and most had been with the firm for many years. On vacation in the 1960s Howard Beard often drove the firm's old blue Commer van delivering orders to customers in surrounding villages, a service which must have operated at a loss. Alders opposite were seedsmen and florists and Percy Hodges, with the firm from boyhood, must have delivered thousands of bouquets to surprised and happy recipients.

Dale Forty's music shop, Trinder's china shop, Mackney's gents outfitters, The Domestic Bazaar and Tapper's furniture store have long gone, and more recent departures include Mence Smith's hardware store, Freeman Hardy & Willis shoe retailers, Foyle's furniture, Hales and Dewhurst butchers and T.P. Anthony's exclusive dress shop.

Shortly before the Second World War the Royal George Hotel was demolished. Its appearance had been ruined when the upper storey was converted into a cinema and the ground floor provided shop premises for Hepworths. Burtons erected an impressive new building in its place and at almost the same time a brand new cinema, The Ritz, was built nearby on the site of the present shopping precinct. Sadly, the Ritz cinema with its popular Cadena Café lasted little over twenty years before being destroyed by fire in 1961. Following Burton's departure some twenty years ago, Fosters were the first occupants, followed by a general household and ironmongery store and currently a store selling toiletries etc.

Three other cafés were to be found in King Street; Tucks Premier café, the largest, aspired to be up market with waitresses dressed in black with little lace caps, whilst West's café was considered rather select. My favourite was Martha's Pantry, next to Barclays bank, where in the 1950s a three-course meal cost 3s (even less for regulars), excellent quality if limited choice. Brown Windsor soup was normally served, and I continued to patronise the café even after an inexperienced waitress tipped the contents into my lap.

Lewis & Godfrey, whose frontage extended along the parade from the present HSBC bank to the corner and some way up Russell Street was Stroud's principal department store, well known throughout the county. The old building was in need of modernisation and this was partially carried out by the Cainscross & Ebley Co-operative Society when they acquired the store around 1960. Since then Mackay's and McIlroy's, their successors, have carried out extensive refurbishment.

Years ago King Street Parade was one of the main bus termini in the town at a time when buses took cinema goers back to their villages after 10 p.m. The current plan to remove buses from the Merrywalks bus station to an interchange by the railway station has reached an impasse, but as the Merrywalks site is soon to be occupied by a rather ambitious multi-screen cinema with no really satisfactory provision for the buses, one wonders what the future holds for public transport in the Stroud valleys.

Above: King Street as seen from the upper floor of the Holloway Building, *c.* 1930. Following its conversion the old Royal George Hotel presents a sorry sight and Hepworth's sun blinds do nothing to enhance its appearance.

Right: PC 'Banger' Yates on point duty near Town Time, *c.* 1930. He was very well known in the town, and the subject of a cartoon by *Echo* Organ the well known caricaturist.

King Street *en fête* for the Silver Jubilee. An ice-cream vendor plies his trade on the left and a double decker is about to depart for Gloucester or Cheltenham.

From the other direction we see the signs for Dale Forty pianos and Tapper house furnisher on the left, with the Bon Marché, Green Dragon and Premier Café on the right, *c.* 1935.

PC 'Banger' Yates on patrol around 1925, watched by two respectful lads. An old Bristol bus is about to leave for Gloucester, presumably via Stonehouse.

A comfortable ride could not be expected in this Whiteshill bus with solid tyres, *c.* 1920. Perhaps that's why there are no passengers!

Above: Two very smart small shops next to WH Smiths, photographed in the late 1930s. Note Bown's name picked out using neon lighting.

Right: Two demure assistants pose reluctantly for the photographer, *c.* 1930. The Domestic Bazaar was a very popular shop selling general household requisites in the pre-war period.

Opposite above: Lewis & Godfrey, Stroud's largest departmental store, seen here around 1940. The AA sign indicates that London is 103¾ miles away!

Opposite below: Apart from two individuals lurking under Hilton's sun blind, King Street Parade looks deserted, *c.* 1938. Edwin Peckham clearly intended that nothing should distract from his portrayal of the shop front.

In this lively photograph a horse and cart manoeuvres through the traffic watched by an alert policeman, *c.* 1935. The Ideal Home Club invites you to climb the stairs with free entry to their great furniture show: 'Walk in and look around no need to buy'.

Mence Smith, the popular hardware store, stands at the corner of Bath Street, *c.* 1960. Alders, Fine Fare and Foyle's are also visible, but who remembers Woodside?

The handsome Burtons building was completed in 1939. Unfortunately the shop frontage has been somewhat defaced by subsequent tenants. Note the unit on the far right that was used as a centre for raising money to put towards the building of warships, *c.* 1940.

Hale's smart new premises decorated for the 1935 Silver Jubilee. Quite a contrast to the Domestic Bazaar who were the previous tenants.

Above: The opening of the Ritz Cinema immediately before the war. Comissionaire and page boy patiently await an influx of patrons.

Left: With evacuees and war workers pouring into the town, the presence of two modern cinemas was a tremendous asset. On Sunday nights concerts were presented at the Ritz, attracting renowned artistes and entertainers as indicated in the programme.

King Street, Stroud.

Above: Shop blinds were once a common, if rather ugly, feature of our streets. The writer of this postcard sent to Caen (Normandy) was clearly intrigued by this display in King Street.

Right: The elaborate façade of The Green Dragon, seen here, was rebuilt by Godsells around 1900. Halfords now occupy the premises, but what happened to the elegant inn sign?.

King Street

	1910	1950	2003
No.			
1	Hill & Sons ironmongers	F.W. Woolworth Ltd	F.W. Woolworth Ltd
2	R. Mitchell furnishers	,,	,,
3	W. Gillman hatter/hosier	Hilton's shoes	Shoezone
4	Royal George Hotel	Burton tailors	Homestyle
5	Gardner & Sons builders	Barlow Pye chemist	Lloyds chemist
6	Smith hairdresser	Freeman Hardy & Willis	Phones 4 U
7		Mence Smith hardware	Card Fair
8	Chew ironmonger	Tuck's Premier Café	Via Sacra/Eclipse
9	Alder seedsman	Alder seedsman	Baker Dolphin travel agent
10	Green Dragon Inn	Green Dragon Inn	Halfords
11	Collins printers	Foyle's furnishers	Oxfam
12	Rufus Weston tailor	Smart's furnishers	Sunshine Food Shop
13	Gardner hatter	Gardner hatter	Andrews estate agnt
14	Arnold gents' outfitter	London Central Meat Co.	Spec Savers
		Pompadours hairdresser	,,
15	WH Smith newsagent	WH Smith newsagent	WH Smith
16	Shepherd dressmaker	Barclay's Bank	Barclay's Bank
17	,,	,,	,,
18	Shelton carvers/guilders	Martha's Pantry	Nationwide Building Society
19	Strange grocer	Strange grocer	Taylors estate agent
20	Anthony draper	Anthony draper	Pine Shop
21	Murphy confectioner	West's Café	Reflections hairdresser
22	Domestic Bazaar	Hale & Sons butcher	Kebab World
23	Tones hatter/hosier	J.M. Stone electrician	Nobel James estate agent
24	Coley chemist	Clark draper	Blockbuster video
25	Park draper/furnisher	Midland Bank	HSBC Bank
26	,,	,,	,,
27	,,	,,	,,
28	Lewis & Godfrey	Lewis & Godfrey	McKay's clothes
29	,,	,,	,,
30	,,	,,	,,

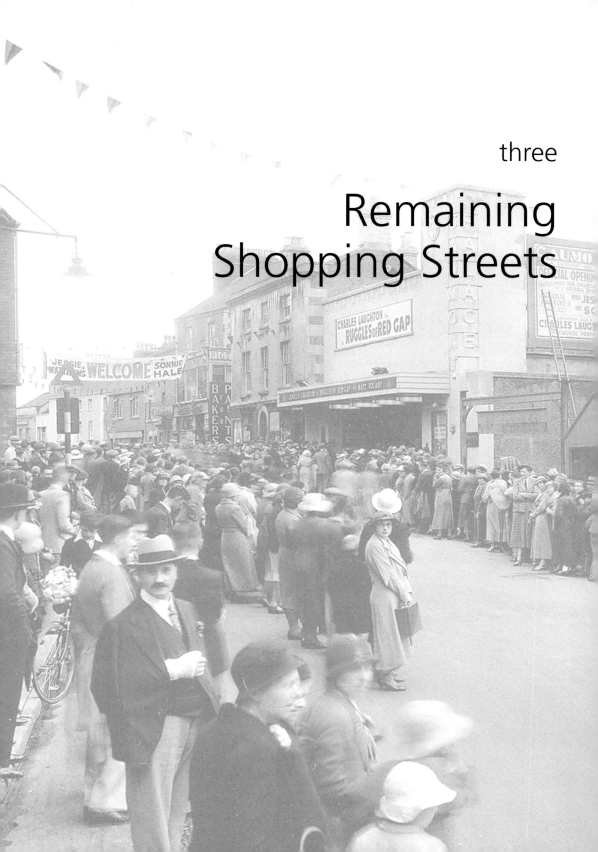

three

Remaining
Shopping Streets

Gloucester Street

This steep northerly approach to the town centre evolved from the former Badbrook Lane which crossed the Slade Brook by means of a ford. Several shops in the lower part of the street, including Plested's High Class Grocery Store, were demolished prior to the widening of Merrywalks.

Before the introduction of one-way systems the crossroads at the top of the street required the presence of a policeman on point duty. No attempt appears to have been made to set back the Greyhound Inn when it was rebuilt by Godsells in traditional style in 1900. This Inn together with the Victoria, lower down, is still functioning, but the Painswick Inn is now a centre providing various activities for young people.

The small yard between these two pubs also served the Gloucester Street Forge and another yard below the Painswick Inn was the location of a small produce and poultry market on Thursdays, so our current farmer's market is not a completely new innovation.

Long before the arrival of Indian and Chinese restaurants, Gloucester Street was noted for its cafés and eating places. Stone's Dining Rooms at No. 9 later became the Hancocks faggot and pea shop. Almost opposite was Heals fish and chip restaurant and Tuck's luncheon dining and tea rooms were situated at No. 20 prior to removal to King Street. Many older residents will recall Roger's excellent café operating on two floors at No. 17, premises later occupied by a Chinese restaurant.

Apart from Plesteds, groceries were provided by Melias and Sugar King, while Buckland supplied meat. Mr W.H. Bishop the fishmonger – 'our carts call on customers' – ceased in business many years ago, and No. 16 now serves as the Rajdoot Tandoori restaurant. Another Indian eatery, Exotica, was previously Edmonds long-established ironmongery (later Merrylees).

Children would gaze enviously at the display in T.G. Halls cycle shop. Names such as Raleigh, Hercules, Chase, Sunbeam and BSA. Bicycles were also sold by Taylor Bros on the corner of Bath Street and Halfords had a small shop just below the Greyhound.

Hutchings the hairdresser occupied No. 7 (wash and brush up 2p) and almost opposite the slightly eccentric Mr Dee had a sweet shop, although he would rather have been a coin dealer!

Opposite above: The speciality of the house is fairly obvious from this display, *c.* 1935. Customers could eat in privacy behind the curtained area.

Opposite below: The Waverly Café (later Roger's) took part in the pre-war *Daily Express* window-dressing competition. The poster on the door asks customers to spend more to create employment.

The top of Gloucester Street around 1935 showing Verney's drab ironmongery shop, Mac Fisheries and part of Harper's greengrocery business.

At the lower end we see Plested's grocery shop, a furniture store and petrol pumps flanking an ornate portal, *c.* 1960.

The old police station (seen here around 1960), originally a private house, was extended in 1908 to include a petty sessional court and has since been replaced by the current unprepossessing building in Parliament Street.

THE NEW CORNER, LANSDOWN, STROUD.

Gloucester Street

No.	1910	1950	2003
1	Painswick Inn	Painswick Inn	Painswick Inn Yard Project
2	,,	,,	,,
3	Inn Yard	Inn Yard	Inn Yard
4	Chapman blacksmith	Chapman blacksmith	
5	Queen Victoria Inn	Queen Victoria Inn	Queen Victoria Inn
6	T. Dangerfield carrier	T. Dangerfield	
7	Hutchings barber	Dorothy Ann fashions	Narcissus picture framers
8	Sylvester hardware	W.C. Mann Ltd jeweller	B & J Homebrew
9	Stone's Dining Rooms	Catherine's Gift Shop	P. Hickman barber
10	Aldridge hardware	Halford's Cycles	Vogue hairdresser
11	Browning Dining Rooms	Hancock's faggots &peas	Citizen Office
12	Greyhound Inn	Greyhound Inn	Greyhound Inn
13	Rufus Weston tailor	Smart's furniture	Sunshine Food Shop
14	,,	,,	,,
15	Miller ironmonger	T.G. Hall Ltd cycles	Ladbrokes
16	Bishop fishmonger	Excelsior Meat Co./ Sugar King	Rajdoot restaurant
17	Browning butcher	Roger's Café	Balti Spice
18	A. Burton jeweller	Melias	Kebab& pizza take away
19	Steele saddler	Robinson's corn stores	Pet Fare animal foods
20	Tuck confectioner	Stroud Tyre Co	Peter James lighting
21	Butcher sports outfitter	Heal fish fryer	*vacant*
22	Ward coal merchant	Edmonds/Merrylees ironmongers	Exotica restaurant
23	Sargeant saddler	Stuckey confectioner	Wywong takeway
24	White confectioner	Barber's shop	Hairways hairdresser
25	Taylor Bros footwear	Taylor Bros elect. goods	Helen G. Fashions
26	Taylor Bros cycle dealer	Stroud Pram & Toy shop	Door Centre
27	H. Plested grocer	H. Plested grocer	S.J.H. Furnishing
28	A. White fruiterer	F.L. Wood greengrocer	*demolished*

Opposite above: A postcard from around 1900 showing the newly-built Greyhound Inn at the top of Gloucester Street.

Opposite below: Smarts' furniture store is seen here on a wet day and is seemingly devoid of customers, *c.* 1960. The showrooms occupied all three floors.

Lansdown

This largely residential road was created around 1860 and includes some of the town's most prestigious buildings. Most prominent is the highly decorative School of Science and Art completed around 1900, which for many years housed the Cowle Museum (now replaced by the Museum In The Park). Across the road next to the public gardens stands the former Temperance Hall, used for many years by the Christian Scientists, but which has recently been converted into a small theatre known as The Space. The ornate building adjoining, a former grammar school, became Stroud Free Library in 1887, but for the last thirty years this facility has been housed in an austere modern building erected alongside.

The road continues past residential property to the remains of Bown's mineral water factory, next to which stands the former Liberal Hall. This building, now residential, was originally a Unitarian church, but has since served as a cinema, public hall and more recently a dancing school. The principal, Miss Barabara Pearce, taught many local youngsters the basics of ballroom dancing back in the 1950s.

The former Labour Exchange opposite now serves as the local RSPCA branch clinic and shop,while the rather decrepit building next door at various times housed a fire engine and an ambulance. The two adjacent semi-detached properties were converted from a synagogue, which served the considerable local Jewish community a century ago. Continuing out of town past premises that once housed a small garage and car hire concern, an old cottage stands next to the site of Little Mill, which in the 1930s housed Dick Reyne's fleet of buses. The proprietor, an Australian, unsurprisingly named his business The Austral Garage,and after his departure the premises became Bellamy's garage, in one corner of which were the dismembered remains of a Flying Flea. The Flying Flea (*Pou de Ciel*) was designed by Frenchman Henri Mignet as a DIY project in 1931. A tiny tandem-wing aeroplane, it could be lethal when flown by a novice.

Returning townwards the shop next to The School of Science and Art originally served as Merrett's photographic studio, my uncle Rayner having been previously in partnership with my father in George Street. Following Rayner's death in 1929 the business was continued by his widow but switched to selling artist's materials in more recent years. From this point as far as the Greyhound Inn are the remaining shops interspersed with premises occupied by solicitors , dentists and accountants. The offices of the *Stroud News and Journal* are also prominent and at No.7a Ward Waterman father and son, the latter an accomplished magician, plied their trade as tailors for very many years.

Opposite above: Presumably a Sunday morning photograph, with not one pedestrian in sight, *c.* 1970.

Opposite below: Looking in the other direction the local newspaper offices seen on the right around 1970 were originally *The Stroud Journal* premises founded in 1854.

Lansdown presents a very smart image in this photograph taken by Fred Major over eighty years ago.

The junction with Locking Hill, *c*. 1970. The houses nearest the camera were demolished for a ring road that was never built.

Bown & Co.'s mineral water factory, *c.* 1910. Much of the building was destroyed in a fire some years ago.

Barbara Pearce's dancing studio in the former Liberal Hall is seen here around 1951. Barbara, centre, sits next to some gentleman, no doubt eminent in the dancing world.

Lansdown

No.	1910	1950	2003
1	Witchell & Sons solicitors	B.J. Owen confectioner	Sew & Co.
2	F.W. & G. Fry auctioneers		Christian Science Reading Room
3	Mrs Pattison servant agency	John Bennett photographer	Robert Smith & Co. solicitors
4	Butcher and Co.	H.J. Hook hairdresser house furnishers	”
			”
5	Miss A. Griffin dressmaker	Stroud Laundry Co.	Hilite Windows
6	*Stroud Journal* Office	*Stroud Journal* Office	*Stroud News and Journal* Office
7	J. Thomas dyer and cleaner	C.E. Birchstationer	Cotswold Sewing Machines
8	S.J. Dudbridge accountants	S.J. Dudbridge	S.J. Dudbridge
9	Stroud Liberal Club	Stroud Mutual Benefit Society	Winterbotham Services
10	W.C. Pridham dentist	Owen & James dentists	Brown dentist
11	Miller & Co. cycle dealers	Merrett photographers	The Art Shop
12	School of Science and Art	School of Science and Art	School of Science and Art

London Road

The old cinema marks the point at which Russell Street merges into London Road. The original Palace Theatre lasted some thirty years before being replaced in 1935 by the new Gaumont, opened in front of a huge crowd by Jessie Matthews and Sonnie Hale. At that time the cinema employed a manager, projectionist, cashier, usherettes, commissionaire and page boy, plus an additional cashier at a small separate ticket office catering for the cheapest seats. It was later renamed the Odeon, then following the acquisition by Mecca, the main auditorium was converted into a bingo hall. It was disconcerting to hear the bingo caller whilst watching a film in what was left of the cinema. The building is currently being converted into a night club.

Thanet House next door, now the Town Council offices, was at one time the premises of Wilkes furniture dealers, who were previously to be found in Kendrick Street or King Street Parade. Baker's adjacent shop, picture framers and decorator's requisites, was most efficiently run by Donald Baker and his staff, but following a change of ownership it speedily succumbed to the out-of-town DIY stores. The offices of Gardner & Sons, highly respected builders, were nearby and most of the opposite side of the road was occupied by Steels Motors who had converted the former Isaac Lendon coachworks into their garage and showroom.

A big event in the 1960s was the building of Hussell's new clothes shop, an ambitious project at the time. Unfortunately the proprietors appear to have overstretched their resources and were forced to close after a comparatively short time and the premises are now used as a Job Centre, charity shop etc.whilst the upstairs has been converted into flats.

The Music Centre, recently closed following Mr Smith's retirement, had occupied the site of the former Sesame Bookshop. The manager of this exclusive establishment was Cyril Orr, a rather forbidding looking gentleman who was also a minor composer. A friend of Delius, he was encouraged in his compositions, which included musical settings of Housman's poems.

Older residents will remember Phillip's ironmongery shop, the Blue China Cupboard and Western Hosiery where assistants repaired stockings in full view of the public. On the corner of what is now Cornhill, Ward's Coal Office was easily identified by the presence of a huge lump of coal mounted outside on a concrete plinth. This relic is in storage at Stroud Museum.

The Brunel Mall is built over what was one of Stroud's first car parks situated next to the former GWR goods yard and sidings. Just beyond, a row of brick buildings culminating in the London Hotel leads to the new Waitrose supermarket. Returning to the town on the right-hand side is Sundial House, a former pub, still retaining its sundial with its sober injunction *Memento Mori*.

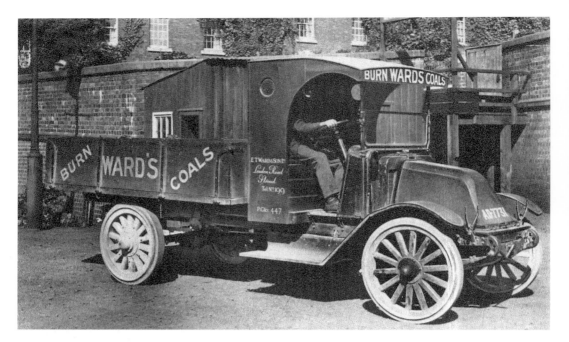

Ward's International coal lorry seen here below Western Buildings (off London Road) around 1920. The largely invisible driver was Charlie Dyer.

The firm's coal office on the corner of London Road and Union Street, *c.* 1970. The huge chunk of anthracite served as a landmark for years, and defied many attempts to chip it away.

Isaac Lendon's coachworks on the corner of John Street with its distinguishing cartwheel set high in the gable. When this photograph was taken most of the premises were occupied by Steels Motors as garage and showroom, *c.* 1960.

A Bristol omnibus double decker waiting outside Rock's Café, one of the many town centre bus stops around 1960.

Left: Hussell's attractive boutique in London Road. Unfortunately their move to grander premises nearby in the 1960s proved unsuccessful.

Below: The Stroud Music Centre in the former Sesame Shop was opened by David Smith and extended as shown in this photograph from around 1957. Mr Smith, a talented musician and organist, has recently retired after forty-seven years here.

London Road

No.	1910	1950	2003
1	Isaac Lendon coach builder	Steels Motors	*Vacant*
2	”	”	Five Star Taxis
3	”	”	Yarnarama
4	”	”	Partridge est agnt
5	Freebury mon.mason	Phillips ironmonger	James & Owen
6		Pritchard tailor	Peter joy estate agent
7		R. Clack elect./radio	Cotswold Appliances
8	James Lee shopkeeper	Blue China Cupboard	Christian Centre
9		Rock's Café	Stroud Secretarial Services
10	Residential	Residential	A.E. Smith solicitors
49	A. Edmond florists	Sesame Shop	Stroud Music Centre
50	A. Jones com. travllr	La Boutique fashions	Murray estate agent
51		O.J. Leach insurance	Cotswold residential letting
52	United Yeast Co. Ltd	Lapage Norris solicitors	Hamptons estate agent
53		Merrymouth Café	”
54	H.T. Pearce blacksmith		Simon David hairdresser
55	Citizen Office	Gardner & Son builder	Norville optician
56	Stone photographer	Western Hosiery	Cotswold Appliances
57	Baker's picture framers	Baker's paints etc.	Job Centre
58	Price florist	Cash Coal Co.	Chatterton Bennett ins.
59	Weston tailor	Thanet House	Stroud Town Council
60	Cinema	Gaumont Cinema	The Warehouse

Rowcroft

The coming of the railway to Stroud around 1845 was a mixed blessing, as the line cut off a section of the town known as Bath Place and also had an adverse effect on the southern approach via Rowcroft. Two stone terraced houses were demolished and the road lowered six feet to provide headroom for what Fisher decribes as an 'ugly railway bridge and the dirty hollow way that passes under it'. The bridge was also a hazard for passengers in open top buses should they not be seated when passing underneath.

Like Lansdown, Rowcroft has its share of solicitors and accountants and for many years provided premises for the Stroud Building Society, Watson the chemist, E.J. Rowell the estate agent and the Merrymouth Café, which was renowned for good English fare. Doctors Hills and Mould, well-known medical practitioners, occupied part of the end terrace nearest to Lloyds Bank in the days when receptionists and practice nurses were largely unknown.

The large building opposite known variously as The Holloway Institute, Conservative and Unionist Club and Red Cross House was erected in 1894. The statue of George Holloway, founder of the Holloway Benefit Society and local industrialist, is a well-known land mark. The former stationmaster's house stands above the high brick wall stretching down to the railway bridge and just below was the public weighbridge with its tiny office built into the bank and only recently demolished.

The large new offices of the Stroud and Swindon Building Society are built on the site of The Stroud Brewery, and many of us not only lament the demise of the fine stone office block and tall 1901 chimney, which dominated the approach to the town, but also the aroma that pervaded the town on brewing days.

Opposite above: Rowcroft appears to have changed little in a hundred years judging by this postcard, *c.* 1910. The children are standing outside the Rowcroft Commercial Temperance Family Hotel.

Opposite below: The offices of the Stroud Brewery (seen here around 1970) and the tall chimney that dominated this approach to the town for many years. Most of the site is now occupied by the Stroud and Swindon Building Society.

Rowcroft, Stroud.

Russell Street

This once popular street has recently suffered from the blight of empty shops. The removal of Boots the Chemist to High Street and the closure of Hurrans (florists and garden requisites) started the rot, but there are now some signs of resurgence. The main post office remains and the original post office building has been converted into a smart public house. The drug store that occupied part of the former Lewis & Godfrey premises no longer greets visitors with a huge display of toilet rolls, and the premises opposite the Shunters (formerly Railway) Inn has been refurbished. The Foresters Arms has long gone, and older residents will recall Captain Barton sporting a brown bowler and tweeds with a red carnation in the button hole, hitching his horse in the pub yard before seeking liquid refreshment in the bar.

Sands, the only quality men's outfitters, has closed after seventy-four years, to become another ladies' hairdressers. Freemans Hatters & Hosiers occupied a small shop next to the post office, and in the back room Mr Preston the barber still retained a display of revolving brushes on shiny brass mountings, relics of Edwardian days. Higher up was Moody the fishmongers one of three such shops in the town, now replaced by a supplier in the Shambles or by the out-of-town supermarkets.

For many years the Wicliffe Motor Co. (which originally specialised in cycles) traded from premises now occupied by Peacocks and opposite, music enthusiasts purchased records and sheet music from Percy Grainger's music shop. James and Owens printers, stationers and bookbinders next to the post office moved to smaller premises in London Road many years ago, and once well-known firms like Wells the jewellers and Pearce the saddler, with distinctive horse head mounted high on the building, are distant memories.

The longest established business still operating is the photographic shop known as Peckhams. In late Victorian times the resident photographer was J.H. Elliott, who was succeeded in 1903 by Henry Comley. Twenty years later the business passed to Reynolds and shortly after that Edwin C. Peckham acquired the premises that still bears his name. Even before Elliott, my father, Mark Merrett, used a photographic studio for many years which was later converted into a workshop by the Art Memorial Company; this was demolished around 1960 following the expansion by Steel's Motors before they in turn were replaced by the Stroud Building Society (now Stroud & Swindon).

Finally, mention must be made of the Saranne Restaurant, which with its fishpond and classical decor brought a touch of glamour to the town. Sadly, like its competitors The Flamingo and 513 Tuckerie, they have all been replaced by the current spread of Indian and Chinese restaurants.

Opposite above: These wooden buildings used by the Art Memorial Company, previously served for many years as Merrett Bros photographic studio, as evidenced by the large skylights, *c.* 1950. The local building society now have their town centre premises here.

Opposite below: Sim's clock erected in 1921 stands at the junction of George Street and Russell Street, *c.* 1930. The one-way system was clearly not in operation at that time.

THE COUNTY STUDIO
STROUD

Edwin E Peckham

ALL AMATEUR SUPPLIES AND SERVICE. CINE
SUPPLIES :: KODASCOPE, PATHESCOPE, ETC.

EDWIN C. PECKHAM
Photographer.   Commercial Specialist
'PHONE 106.

Above: The opening in 1935 of the new Gaumont Cinema by Jessie Matthews and Sonnie Hale was obviously a big occasion and the road has been cleared of spectators for the stars' arrival. A nightclub will shortly open in the former cinema.

Left: A pre-war Peckham advert. The firm has been in business in Russell Street for some eighty years.

Opposite above: The Wicliffe Motor Company founded in 1913 originally sold bicycles, seen here *c.* 1950. Following conversion to an International Stores mini-market the premises are now occupied by Peacocks.

Opposite below: Boots The Chemists occupied this corner for many years and their removal to the High Street left a gap yet to be filled, *c.* 1960. The old shop operated a lending library on the upper floor and also sold books, gramophone records, gifts and stationery. Miss Eileen Haliday was employed by the firm for forty-seven years and in her capacity as dispenser must have met the majority of the townsfolk.

Russell Street

No.	1910	1950	2003
1	Lewis & Godfrey drapers	Lewis & Godfrey drapers	McKay's clothing
2	"	"	"
3	Railway Hotel	Railway Hotel	Shunters Inn
4	Foresters Arms	Foresters Arms	*vacant*
	Wilts & Dorset Bank	Nat. Provincial Bank	Nat West Bank
5	Billett & Co. hatters	Sands outfitters	Sands outfitters
6	Browning fruiterer/	Grainger music	Victoria Wine
	Art Memorial Co./	Steels Motors	Stroud & Swindon
	Merrett Bros photographer	"	Building Society
7	Wells jewellers	Wells jewellers	"
8	Parker & Co. dyers	Parker & Co. dyers	Ladbrookes
9	Pearce saddler	Pearce saddler	Travail employment
			agent
10	Comley photographer	Peckham photographer	Peckham photographer
11	Smith Rogers pork butcher	Wicliffe Motors	Peacocks clothes
12	Wicliffe cycles	"	H K House
13	Moody fishmonger	Moody fishmonger	Milano's Pizzas
14	James printer	James & Owen printers	Post Office
15	*Gloucestershire Echo* office	"	"
16	General Post Office	General Post Office	Lord John Pub
17	Dickenson & Cox coal	Lambert & Cox coal	*vacant*
18	Ricketts confectioner	S.A. Walton & Co.	*vacant*
19	Daniels Bricklayers Arms	seedsman	*vacant*
20	Freeman hatter /hosier	Freeman hatter/hosier	USA Chicken
21	Temperance Hotel	Woodford tobacconist	*vacant*
22	Boots chemist	Boots chemist	*vacant*
23	"	"	"
24	Holloway Institute	Holloway Institute	Holloway Institute
25	"	"	"
26	"	"	"

four

Minor Streets

Bath Street

Largely absorbed by the Merrywalks Shopping Precinct this minor street provided a short cut from King Street to the Public Baths, passing Tuck's Premier Hall and bakery and the Exclusive Brethren Meeting Room en route. The Premier Hall, a rather undistinguished building boasting a sprung floor was a well-used amenity advertised as suitable for parties, dances or whist drives, with or without orchestra.

The Meeting Room was a simple stone building used by the Plymouth Brethren, who held a weekly bible class here and it is recalled that this was often led by a Colonel Beckett who travelled all the way from Cheltenham on horseback. Much more recently William Knight, a skilled sheet-metal worker, and Dick Baxter, a well-known plumber, used the building as a workshop, continuing to work into their eighties.

The Public Baths at the bottom of the street, constructed in 1896 and recently demolished, were certainly an improvement on the Wallbridge canal lock for swimmers, and the slipper baths providing hot water, soap and towel must have been a valuable amenity. Clarence Cull, the superintendent and a fine swimmer was a keen supporter of the Stroud Show and enjoyed displaying his physique in the carnival procession dressed as a Roman centurion or African chief.

The Door, a young person's meeting place, occupies buildings vacated by Poole's fruit and vegetable market and a former insurance office.

Opposite above: This section of Bath Street now forms part of the Merrywalks precinct. The Premier Hall emergency exit is seen on the left, *c.* 1970.

Opposite below: The lower end of Bath Street, *c.* 1970. The former Brethren Meeting Room is just behind the two figures in the distance.

Bedford Street

Lord John Russell, son of the Duke of Bedford, certainly left his mark on Stroud. This street together with John Street and Russell Street was named in honour of the former Stroud MP who became Prime Minister in 1863.

The Stroud Dispensary erected in 1755 stood on the corner of Bedford Street and George Street and was joined by a casualty hospital in 1835.

The Congregational church with its distinctive cupola was built in 1837, as the Old Chapel was proving inadequate for the large congregations. During the Second World War the large schoolroom was converted into a canteen for evacuees and later served war workers as a British Restaurant, finally closing in 1949.

The adjacent open space, now used for trade access and disabled parking, was the site of the Town Flour Mills. The decorative letterhead used by Fawkes Bros Hay, Corn, Seed and Cake Merchants included the artist's much exaggerated depiction of the premises.

Burger Star and the public conveniences now occupy the site of Bedford House, formerly the offices of Mr R.E. Stuart who, when aged over ninety, was the oldest practicing solicitor in the country. He appears to have been a colourful character who, in his capacity as Clerk to the Board of Governors at the Wheatenhurst Union Workhouse,would often arrive on horseback. One of his articled pupils who reached high office in the judiciary periodically visited Stuart and always addressed him deferentially as 'Sir'.

Mother Nature, the well-known healthfood shop and restaurant, has been established in Bedford Street for many years and offers an alternative menu to Burger Star opposite.

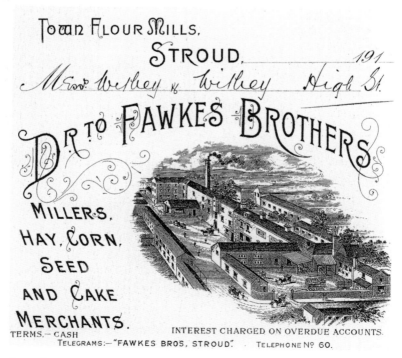

A Fawkes Bros letterhead from 1911.

John Street

The principle building in this minor street is the Baptist Chapel built in 1824, which still attracts a good congregation. Although outwardly it presents a rather plain appearance, the galleried interior is quite impressive.

Following the demolition of the distinctive Isaac Lendon coachworks on the corner of London Road, and its replacement by small shop units, a number of retailers have come and gone, including Metro Colour who operated a fast and efficient photographic service.

The site of the old clothing factory on the corner of John Street and Union Street has been redeveloped and includes a sizeable shop selling beds, divans and suchlike.

Much of the original Holloways factory was destroyed by fire in 1973. This is a view of the damage seen from John Street.

The John Street Hall alias The Empire Club became the local headquarters of the British Union of Fascists, and received a visit from Sir Oswald Mosley (in centre) in 1934. The premises are now used by a furniture recycling organisation.

G. Jurisch, *Hairdresser and . . . Perfumer.*

From London, Paris, etc.

First=class
Ladies' and Gents' Haircutting Rooms.

Agent for Sprocks' Razors
and Dr. Wilson's Hair Restorer.

Great variety of French and English Perfumery and all Toilet Requisites.

Combings made up.   Theatrical Wigs on hire.

ALL KINDS OF
ARTISTIC HAIR-WORK Executed on the Premises.

John Street, (Late Kendrick St.) **STROUD.**

115

Above left: Jurisch hairdressing establishment has since had a variety of occupants including greengrocers, but currently is a shop selling antiques and bric-à-brac.

Above right: The red-brick factory building used for many years as the offices of the Stroud Rural District Council is seen here shortly before demolition in the 1980s.

Threadneedle Street

Part of a thoroughfare running from the top of High Street to Bedford Street, the widest section, is known as Threadneedle Street, the name deriving from the original Holloway's clothing factory that flanked the street. One side of the street has been completely redeveloped following a disasterous fire in which one life was lost. A number of new shops are located here; but Walker's bakery remains, with its popular Old Lady Café, affording excellent views over the adjacent roof tops.

Above: Threadneedle Street presenting a smart new image following redevelopment.

Left: Threadneedle Street looking towards Kendrick Street shortly after the 1973 fire.

Swan Lane

Once known as Swan Street, this short thoroughfare connects Union Street with High Street near the Medieval Hall. Smith's umbrella shop was located here for many years next to Bill Knight's sheet–metal works.

Swan Lane in August 1967. The lad is passing Pritchard's former slaughter house, with Knight's sheet metal works on the right and Smith's umbrella shop just beyond.

Union Street

Linking High Street with London Road, the original section of the street between the Swan Inn and the former George Inn has been cobbled and pedestrianised. Although narrow, it provided the main starting point for the London-bound stage coaches. The distinctive Swan Inn gallows sign had disappeared at the time of writing, temporarily one hopes.

The children's bookshop with its distinctive windows was formerly a dairy and a grocery store run by a Mrs Beak. Mrs Jones in the adjoining shop eked out a meagre living selling dated sweets and fizzy cordial called Vantas. The two ladies were at loggerheads and children would delight in hearing Mrs Beak's disdainful comments about her neighbour, before calling next door and evoking Mrs Jones' colourful opinion of Mrs Beak.

Now obliterated by the Cornhill development the popular Cotswold Café on the corner of Threadneedle Street was always busy, and was home to a bookmakers, which I believe at one time was an ice-cream business run by Mazucchi. Opposite was Niblett's Mineral Water factory and lower down the Pelican Inn has reverted to its original name, The Union, renowned at one time for its Men Only bar.

In the 1950s the garden area behind the Union provided Stroud's first Berni Inn steak bar, a highly popular venue. The old brick building opposite the Union was the Baptist Sunday School, and the austere building adjoining was formerly the register office and the board room of the guardians of the Stroud Poor Law Union.

The Swan Inn is largely unchanged since this photograph was taken around 1910. The building on the left comprised part of The George Inn, but more recently became S. & R. Ball's extensive wholesale and retail greengrocery business.

Conclusion

No doubt the photographs in this book will have evoked many memories of the days when Stroud (apart from the hills) was a shopper's delight.

The changes over the last fifty years have been dramatic. A mobile population demands the choice and convenience offered by out-of-town superstores, and most town centre food shops have long disappeared. Today's much-improved standard of living and home ownership is reflected by the proliferation of estate agents, travel agents, hairdressers and fast food outlets. Clothes are quickly discarded as fashions change and charity shops reap the benefit. The old 'spit and sawdust' pub is virtually a thing of the past, and many people either drink at home or prefer to travel to an out-of-town pub/restaurant.

Fortunately, Stroud still has a number of independent traders offering a wide variety of goods in contrast to the multiples with their stereotyped frontages often completely at variance with the architecture of the building they occupy.

More recently the markets at Cornhill and The Shambles have proved most popular with shoppers who appreciate the quality and value of goods offered. These markets increase the footfall in the town centre and the lively atmosphere generated is so reminiscent of pre-war days when market traders sold their wares from stalls on The Cross.

Stroud's main retailers

Trade	1910	1950	2003
Amusement Arcade			2
Antiques s/h furniture	4	2	3
Art materials		1	1
Bacon curer/pork butcher	2	2	
Baker/confectioner	5	7	2
Bank	2	4	5
Barber/hairdresser	5	11	9
Blacksmith	2	1	
Bookmaker		2	3
Bookshop/ephemera		1	4
Butcher	8	12	
Card shop			3
Carpet shop		1	1
Catalogue shop			1
Charity shop			7
Chemist	5	6	4
China/glass	4	1	
Clothing general			7
Cinema	1	2	
Clothing children	1	2	
Cobbler	2	2	1
Computer requisites			1
Cycle agent	4	3	1
Dairy	1	2	
Dentist	3	4	6
Departmental stores	1	3	1
Decorators supplies	1	2	
Domestic supplies	1		
Dressmaker	3		
Draper	10	7	1
Dry cleaners/dyers	2	3	1

Trade	1910	1950	2003
Electrical/radio/TV		11	2
Fancy goods/ethnic	3	2	7
Fish fryers		5	3
Fishmonger	3	5	1
Florist	4	1	2
Footwear	8	9	2
Furniture/beds	6	3	2
Grocer	14	12	2
General store	1	2	2
Gent's outfitters	3	7	2
Greengrocer/fruiterer	4	7	2
Hardware	2	1	
Health clinic			3
Health store		1	2
Hatter/hosier	5	2	
Insurance agency		4	2
Internet café			1
Sewing machines	1	1	1
Sports items/camping	1	1	3
Sweet shop	3	3	1
Take away foods			7
Tailor	9	5	1
Tobacconist	4	3	
Travel agent		1	5
Tyre supplier		1	
Umbrella maker	1	1	
Video shop			2
Wines and spirits	1	1	1
Woolshop		2	2
White goods (fridges etc.)		2	1

Stroud Pubs 1903

Pub	Location	Operating
Anchor	Bath Rd	closed
Bedford Arms	High St	closed
Bell Inn	Wallbridge	operating 2003
Bisley House	Middle St	operating 2003
Bricklayers Arms	Russell St	closed
Butcher's Arms	Parliament St	demolished
Butcher's Arms	Acre St	closed
Clothiers	Bath Rd	operating 2003
Coopers Arms	*not known*	*not known*
Corn Exchange	High St	demolished
Corn Hall	Shambles	closed
Cross Hands	Summer St	operating 2003
Cross Keys	Acre St	*not known*
Crown & Sceptre	Horns Rd	operating 2003
Crown Inn	High St	demolished
Duke of York	Nelson St	operating 2003
Foresters	Russell St	closed
Fountain	Slad Rd	operating 2003
Globe	L/Leazes	*not known*
Golden Fleece	Nelson St	operating 2003
Green Dragon	King St	closed
Grey Hound	Gloucester St	operating 2003
Half Moon	Hill St	closed
Hope Inn	Cainscross Rd	demolished
Horse & Groom	Leazes	closed
Imperial Hotel	Station Rd	operating 2003
King's Arms	Wallbridge	demolished
King's Head	Cross	demolished
Lamb	Church St	closed
Leopard	Parliament St	demolished
Masons	Gloucester St	closed
Nelson	High St	closed
New Inn	Hill St	demolished
New Inn	Lower St	closed
Oddfellows	Summer St	closed
Orange Tree	Hill St	demolished
Painswick	Gloucester St	closed
Plough	Union St	demolished
Post Office	George St	closed
Prince of Wales	Slad Rd	closed
Railway (Shunters)	Russell St	operating 2003
Red Lion	Summer St	*not known*

Pub	Location	Operating
Rising Sun	Nelson St	closed
Royal George	King St	demolished
Ship	Uplands	*not known*
Spread Eagle	Bisley Rd	demolished
Star	Hill St	demolished
Sundial	London Rd	closed
Swan	Union St	operating 2003
Target	Bisley Rd	closed
Union	Union St	operating 2003
Victoria	Gloucester St	operating 2003
Wellington Arms	Nelson St	closed
White Lion	High St	closed
Lord John	Russell St	New *c.* 2000

Approximate number of pubs 1903 = 54
Number today (2004) = 15

James Dean, *mein host* at the Hope Inn, Wallbridge, seen here around 1960.

Other local titles published by Tempus

Cheltenham Volume II
ELAINE HEASMAN

Comprising over 230 rare images, this volume provides a glimpse into the history of Cheltenham during the last 150 years. Included are many of Cheltenham's well-known landmarks, such as the elegant Promenade and the Queen's Hotel, as well as surrounding areas such as Charlton Kings, Prestbury and Leckhampton. Also pictured are the families who have traded for generations and individual personalities who will be remembered by many.
0 7524 3085 8

Haunted Gloucester
EILEEN FRY AND ROSEMARY HARVEY

This enthralling selection recalls strange and spooky happenings in the city's ancient streets, churches, theatres and public houses, including The Kingsholm Inn and Bridge Inn! From paranormal manifestations at Gloucester Docks to the ghostly activity of a monk who is said to haunt the city's twelfth-century cathedral, this spine-tingling collection of supernatural tales is sure to appeal to anyone interested in Gloucester's haunted heritage.
0 7524 3312 1

The Royal Family in Gloucestershire
MICHAEL CHARITY

Gloucestershire is popular with the Royal family. There are Royal residences there – Highgrove, Gatcombe, Badminton, Lypiatt Manor – and social events, such as The Cheltenham Gold Cup and the Badminton horse trials. The Royal family's associations with Gloucestershire over the years are captured here in Michael Charity's photographs.
0 7524 2871 3

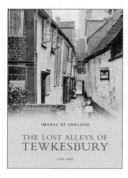

The Lost Alleys of Tewkesbury
CLIFF BURD

The lost alleys of Tewkesbury are a fascinating subject for research. Some carry the name of a pub, many are a reminder of families who lived there and others reflect the occupation of the residents. These alleys, the people who lived, worked and eventually died there, are the story of the town itself. They reflect its growth, its industry, its fortunes and misfortunes, and recreate a sense of Tewkesbury past.
0 7524 3189 7

If you are interested in purchasing other books published by Tempus, or in case you have difficulty finding any Tempus books in your local bookshop, you can also place orders directly through our website
www.tempus-publishing.com